SELECTED CANTOS OF EZRA POUND

The Cantos of Ezra Pound

The Fourth Canto (1919)
A Draft of XVI Cantos (1925)
A Draft of the Cantos 17-27 (1928)
A Draft of XXX Cantos (1930)
Eleven New Cantos XXXI-XLI (1934)
The Fifth Decad of Cantos (1937)
Cantos LII-LXXI (1940)
The Pisan Cantos (1948)
Section: Rock-Drill de los Cantares 85-95 (1955)
Thrones 96-106 de los Cantares (1959)
Drafts & Fragments of Cantos CX-CXVII (1968)
Cantos I-CXVII (1970)
Canto CXX (1972)

SELECTED CANTOS OF EZRA POUND

A NEW DIRECTIONS BOOK

Typographic design by Giovanni Mardersteig

Manufactured in the United States of America

Published in Canada by George J. McLeod, Ltd., Toronto.

New Directions Books are published for James Laughlin
by New Directions Publishing Corporation,
80 Eighth Avenue, New York 10011

NINTH PRINTING

To Olga Rudge

'Tempus loquendi'

CONTENTS

FOREWORD   1

DRAFT OF XXX CANTOS   3

JEFFERSON — NUEVO MUNDO   37

SIENA — THE LEOPOLDINE REFORMS   43

CHINESE CANTOS — JOHN ADAMS   59

THE PISAN CANTOS   79

SECTION: ROCK-DRILL   96

THRONES   103

DRAFTS & FRAGMENTS OF CANTOS CX-CXVII   116

FOREWORD

I have made these selections to indicate main elements in the *Cantos*. To the specialist the task of explaining them. As Jung says: "Being essentially the instrument for his work, he [the artist] is subordinate to it and we have no reason for expecting him to interpret it for us. He has done the best that is in him by giving it form and he must leave interpretation to others and to the future."

The best introduction to the *Cantos* and to the present selection of passages might be the following lines from the earlier draft of a Canto (1912), reprinted in the fiftieth memorial issue of *Poetry* (Chicago).

> Hang it all, there can be but one "Sordello"!
> But say I want to, say I take your whole bag of tricks,
> Let in your quirks and tweeks, and say the thing's an art-form,
> Your Sordello, and that the modern world
> Needs such a rag-bag to stuff all its thoughts in;
> Say that I dump my catch, shiny and silvery
> As fresh sardines slapping and slipping on the marginal cobbles?
> (I stand before the booth, the speech; but the truth
> Is inside this discourse—this booth is full of the marrow of wisdom.)

EZRA POUND

Venice, 20th October, 1966

PUBLISHER'S NOTE

The basic selection for this book was made by Ezra Pound in September, 1966, and it was first published in London by Faber & Faber in 1967. In this American edition, which was composed in Monotype Bembo, in the style of the Mardersteig first printings of *The Pisan Cantos*, *Section Rock-Drill* and *Thrones*, the more compressed setting making a few extra pages available, the following passages were added by the publisher:

1. *Canto LII*. The section based on Lü Shih's *Spring and Autumn* was completed by the addition of 78 lines, to the end of the Canto.

2. The first 107 lines of *Canto LXXXIII*.

3. The fragment of *Canto CXV* and *Canto CXVI* from *Drafts & Fragments of Cantos CX-CXVII* which were first published in book form in 1969.

J. L.

CANTO I

And then went down to the ship,
Set keel to breakers, forth on the godly sea, and
We set up mast and sail on that swart ship,
Bore sheep aboard her, and our bodies also
Heavy with weeping, and winds from sternward
Bore us out onward with bellying canvas,
Circe's this craft, the trim-coifed goddess.
Then sat we amidships, wind jamming the tiller,
Thus with stretched sail, we went over sea till day's end.
Sun to his slumber, shadows o'er all the ocean,
Came we then to the bounds of deepest water,
To the Kimmerian lands, and peopled cities
Covered with close-webbed mist, unpierced ever
With glitter of sun-rays
Nor with stars stretched, nor looking back from heaven
Swartest night stretched over wretched men there.
The ocean flowing backward, came we then to the place
Aforesaid by Circe.
Here did they rites, Perimedes and Eurylochus,
And drawing sword from my hip
I dug the ell-square pitkin;
Poured we libations unto each the dead,
First mead and then sweet wine, water mixed with white flour.
Then prayed I many a prayer to the sickly death's-heads;
As set in Ithaca, sterile bulls of the best
For sacrifice, heaping the pyre with goods,

A sheep to Tiresias only, black and a bell-sheep.
Dark blood flowed in the fosse,
Souls out of Erebus, cadaverous dead, of brides
Of youths and of the old who had borne much;
Souls stained with recent tears, girls tender,
Men many, mauled with bronze lance heads,
Battle spoil, bearing yet dreory arms,
These many crowded about me; with shouting,
Pallor upon me, cried to my men for more beasts;
Slaughtered the herds, sheep slain of bronze;
Poured ointment, cried to the gods,
To Pluto the strong, and praised Proserpine;
Unsheathed the narrow sword,
I sat to keep off the impetuous impotent dead,
Till I should hear Tiresias.
But first Elpenor came, our friend Elpenor,
Unburied, cast on the wide earth,
Limbs that we left in the house of Circe,
Unwept, unwrapped in sepulchre, since toils urged other.
Pitiful spirit. And I cried in hurried speech:
"Elpenor, how art thou come to this dark coast?
Cam'st thou afoot, outstripping seamen?"

And he in heavy speech:
"Ill fate and abundant wine. I slept in Circe's ingle.
Going down the long ladder unguarded,
I fell against the buttress,
Shattered the nape-nerve, the soul sought Avernus.
But thou, O King, I bid remember me, unwept, unburied,
Heap up mine arms, be tomb by sea-bord, and inscribed:

A man of no fortune, and with a name to come.
And set my oar up, that I swung mid fellows."

And Anticlea came, whom I beat off, and then Tiresias Theban,
Holding his golden wand, knew me, and spoke first:
"A second time? why? man of ill star,
Facing the sunless dead and this joyless region?
Stand from the fosse, leave me my bloody bever
For soothsay."
                    And I stepped back,
And he strong with the blood, said then: "Odysseus
Shalt return through spiteful Neptune, over dark seas,
Lose all companions." And then Anticlea came.
Lie quiet Divus. I mean, that is Andreas Divus,
In officina Wecheli, 1538, out of Homer.
And he sailed, by Sirens and thence outward and away
And unto Circe.
                    Venerandam,
In the Cretan's phrase, with the golden crown, Aphrodite,
Cypri munimenta sortita est, mirthful, orichalchi, with golden
Girdles and breast bands, thou with dark eyelids
Bearing the golden bough of Argicida. So that:

Palace in smoky light,
Troy but a heap of smouldering boundary stones,
ANAXIFORMINGES! Aurunculeia!
Hear me. Cadmus of Golden Prows!
The silver mirrors catch the bright stones and flare,
Dawn, to our waking, drifts in the green cool light;
Dew-haze blurs, in the grass, pale ankles moving.
Beat, beat, whirr, thud, in the soft turf
           under the apple trees,
Choros nympharum, goat-foot, with the pale foot alternate;
Crescent of blue-shot waters, green-gold in the shallows,
A black cock crows in the sea-foam;

And by the curved, carved foot of the couch,
           claw-foot and lion head, an old man seated
Speaking in the low drone . . . :
                Ityn!
Et ter flebiliter, Ityn, Ityn!
And she went toward the window and cast her down,
           "All the while, the while, swallows crying:
Ityn!
           It is Cabestan's heart in the dish."
           "It is Cabestan's heart in the dish?
           No other taste shall change this."
And she went toward the window,
                the slim white stone bar
Making a double arch;

6

Firm even fingers held to the firm pale stone;
Swung for a moment,
                    and the wind out of Rhodez
Caught in the full of her sleeve.
            . . . the swallows crying:
'Tis. 'Tis. Ytis!
            Actæon . . .
                and a valley,
The valley is thick with leaves, with leaves, the trees,
The sunlight glitters, glitters a-top,
Like a fish-scale roof,
            Like the church roof in Poictiers
If it were gold.
            Beneath it, beneath it
Not a ray, not a sliver, not a spare disc of sunlight
Flaking the black, soft water;
Bathing the body of nymphs, of nymphs, and Diana,
Nymphs, white-gathered about her, and the air, air.
Shaking, air alight with the goddess,
            fanning their hair in the dark,
Lifting, lifting and waffing:
Ivory dipping in silver,
            Shadow'd, o'ershadow'd
Ivory dipping in silver,
Not a splotch, not a lost shatter of sunlight.
Then Actæon: Vidal,
Vidal. It is old Vidal speaking,
            stumbling along in the wood,
Not a patch, not a lost shimmer of sunlight,
            the pale hair of the goddess.

7

The dogs leap on Actæon,
                "Hither, hither, Actæon,"
Spotted stag of the wood;
Gold, gold, a sheaf of hair,
                Thick like a wheat swath,
Blaze, blaze in the sun,
                The dogs leap on Actæon.
Stumbling, stumbling along in the wood,
Muttering, muttering Ovid:
                "Pergusa . . . pool . . . pool . . . Gargaphia,
"Pool . . . pool of Salmacis."
                The empty armour shakes as the cygnet moves.

Thus the light rains, thus pours, *e lo soleills plovil*
The liquid and rushing crystal
                beneath the knees of the gods.
Ply over ply, thin glitter of water;
Brook film bearing white petals.
The pine at Takasago
                grows with the pine of Isé!
The water whirls up the bright pale sand in the spring's mouth
"Behold the Tree of the Visages!"
Forked branch-tips, flaming as if with lotus.
                Ply over ply
The shallow eddying fluid,
                beneath the knees of the gods.

Torches melt in the glare
                set flame of the corner cook-stall,
Blue agᐃte casing the sky (as at Gourdon that time)

the sputter of resin,
Saffron sandal so petals the narrow foot: Hymenæus Io!
          Hymen, Io Hymenæe! Aurunculeia!
One scarlet flower is cast on the blanch-white stone.

          And Sō-Gyoku, saying:
"This wind, sire, is the king's wind,
          This wind is wind of the palace,
Shaking imperial water-jets."
          And Hsiang, opening his collar:
"This wind roars in the earth's bag,
          it lays the water with rushes."
No wind is the king's wind.
          Let every cow keep her calf.
"This wind is held in gauze curtains . . ."
          No wind is the king's . . .

The camel drivers sit in the turn of the stairs,
          Look down on Ecbatan of plotted streets,
"Danaë! Danaë!
          What wind is the king's?"
Smoke hangs on the stream,
The peach-trees shed bright leaves in the water,
Sound drifts in the evening haze,
          The bark scrapes at the ford,
Gilt rafters above black water,
          Three steps in an open field,
Gray stone-posts leading . . .

Père Henri Jacques would speak with the Sennin, on Rokku,
Mount Rokku between the rock and the cedars,

Polhonac,
As Gyges on Thracian platter set the feast,
Cabestan, Tereus,
        It is Cabestan's heart in the dish,
Vidal, or Ecbatan, upon the gilded tower in Ecbatan
Lay the god's bride, lay ever, waiting the golden rain.
By Garonne. "Saave!"
The Garonne is thick like paint,
Procession, — "Et sa'ave, sa'ave, sa'ave Regina!" —
Moves like a worm, in the crowd.
Adige, thin film of images,
Across the Adige, by Stefano, Madonna in hortulo,
As Cavalcanti had seen her.
        The Centaur's heel plants in the earth loam.
And we sit here . . .
        there in the arena . . .

CANTO IX

One year floods rose,
One year they fought in the snows,
One year hail fell, breaking the trees and walls.
Down here in the marsh they trapped him in one year,
And he stood in the water up to his neck
         to keep the hounds off him,
And he floundered about in the marsh
         and came in after three days,
That was Astorre Manfredi of Faenza
         who worked the ambush
         and set the dogs off to find him,
In the marsh, down here under Mantua,
And he fought in Fano, in a street fight,
         and that was nearly the end of him;
And the Emperor came down and knighted us,
And they had a wooden castle set up for fiesta,
And one year Basinio went out into the courtyard
         Where the lists were, and the palisades
         had been set for the tourneys,
And he talked down the anti-Hellene,
         And there was an heir male to the seignor,
         And Madame Ginevra died.
And he, Sigismundo, was Capitan for the Venetians.
And he had sold off small castles
         and built the great Rocca to his plan,
And he fought like ten devils at Monteluro
         and got nothing but the victory

And old Sforza bitched us at Pesaro;
          (*sic*) March the 16th:
"that Messire Alessandro Sforza
          is become lord of Pesaro
through the wangle of the Illus. Sgr. Mr. Fedricho d'Orbino
Who worked the wangle with Galeaz
          through the wiggling of Messer Francesco,
Who waggled it so that Galeaz should sell Pesaro
          to Alex and Fossembrone to Feddy;
and he hadn't the right to sell.
And this he did *bestialmente*; that is Sforza did *bestialmente*
as he had promised him, Sigismundo, *per capitoli*
          to see that he, Malatesta, should have Pesaro"
And this cut us off from our south half
          and finished our game, thus, in the beginning,
And he, Sigismundo, spoke his mind to Francesco
          and we drove them out of the Marches.

And the King o' Ragona, Alphonse le roy d'Aragon,
          was the next nail in our coffin,
And all you can say is, anyway,
that he Sigismundo called a town council
And Valturio said "as well for a sheep as a lamb"
          and this change-over (*haec traditio*)
As old bladder said *"rem eorum saluavit"*
Saved the Florentine state; and that, maybe, was something.
And "Florence our natural ally" as they said in the meeting
          for whatever that was worth afterward.
And he began building the TEMPIO,
          and Polixena, his second wife, died.

And the Venetians sent down an ambassador
And said "speak humanely,
But tell him it's no time for raising his pay."
And the Venetians sent down an ambassador
      with three pages of secret instructions
To the effect: Did he think the campaign was a joy-ride?
And old Wattle-wattle slipped into Milan
But he couldn't stand Sidg being so high with the Venetians
And he talked it over with Feddy; and Feddy said "Pesaro"
And old Foscari wrote "*Caro mio*
If we split with Francesco you can have it
And we'll help you in every way possible."
      But Feddy offered it sooner.
And Sigismundo got up a few arches,
And stole that marble in Classe, "stole" that is,
Casus est talis:

      Foscari doge, to the prefect of Ravenna
"Why, what, which, thunder, damnation????"

Casus est talis:
      Filippo, commendatary of the *abbazia*
Of Sant Apollinaire, Classe, Cardinal of Bologna
That he did one night (*quadam nocte*) sell to the
Illmo D°, D° Sigismund Malatesta
Lord of Ariminum, marble, porphyry, serpentine,
Whose men, Sigismundo's, came with more than an hundred
two-wheeled ox carts and deported, for the beautifying
of the *tempio* where was Santa Maria in Trivio
Where the same are now on the walls. Four hundred
ducats to be paid back to the *abbazia* by the said swindling

Cardinal or his heirs.
        grnnh! rrnnh, pthg.
Wheels, plaustra, oxen under night-shield,
And on the 13th of August: Aloysius Purtheo,
The next abbot, to Sigismundo, receipt for 200 ducats
Corn-salve for the damage done in that scurry.

And there was the row about that German-Burgundian female
And it was his messianic year, Poliorcetes,
        but he was being a bit too POLUMETIS
And the Venetians wouldn't give him six months vacation.

And he went down to the old brick heap of Pesaro
        and waited for Feddy
And Feddy finally said "I am coming! . . .
        . . . to help Alessandro."
And he said: "This time Mister Feddy has done it."
He said: "Broglio, I'm the goat. This time
        Mr. Feddy has done it (*m'l'ha calata*)."
And he'd lost his job with the Venetians,
And the stone didn't come in from Istria:
And we sent men to the Silk War;
And Wattle never paid up on the nail
        Though we signed on with Milan and Florence;
And he set up the bombards in muck down by Vada
        where nobody else could have set' em
        and he took the wood out of the bombs
        and made 'em of two scoops of metal
And the jobs getting smaller and smaller,
        Until he signed on with Siena;

And that time they grabbed his post-bag.
And what was it, anyhow?
Pitigliano, a man with a ten-acre lot,
Two lumps of tufa,
and they'd taken his pasture land from him,
And Sidg had got back their horses,
and he had two big lumps of tufa
with six hundred pigs in the basements.
And the poor devils were dying of cold.
And this is what they found in the post-bag:
Ex Arimino die xxii Decembris
"*Magnifice ac potens domine, mi singularissime*
I advise yr. Lordship how
I have been with master Alwidge who
has shown me the design of the nave that goes in the middle,
of the church and the design for the roof and . . ."
JHesus,
Magnifico exso. Signor mio
Sence to-day I am recommanded that I have to tel you my father's
opinium that he has shode to Mr. Genare about the valts of the
cherch . . . etc . . .
    Giovane of Master alwise P. S. I think it advisabl that I shud go to
rome to talk to mister Albert so as I can no what he thinks about it
rite.

    Sagramoro . . ."

"*Illustre signor mio*, Messire Battista . . ."

"First: Ten slabs best red, seven by 15, by one third,
Eight ditto, good red, 15 by one,

15

Six of same, 15 by one by one.

Eight columns 15 by three and one third etc . . .

     with carriage, danars 151 . . ."

"MONSEIGNEUR:

Madame Isotta has had me write today about Sr. Galeazzo's daughter. The man who said young pullets make thin soup, knew what he was talking about. We went to see the girl the other day, for all the good that did, and she denied the whole matter and kept her end up without losing her temper. I think Madame Ixotta very nearly exhausted the matter. *Mi pare che avea decto hogni chossia.* All the children are well. Where you are everyone is pleased and happy because of your taking the chateau here we are the reverse as you might say drifting without a rudder. Madame Lucrezia has probably, or should have, written to you, I suppose you have the letter by now. Everyone wants to be remembered to you.   21 Dec. D. de M."

". . . *sagramoro* to put up the derricks. There is a supply of beams at . . ."

"MAGNIFICENT LORD WITH DUE REVERENCE:

Messire Malatesta is well and asks for you every day. He is so much pleased with his pony, It wd. take me a month to write you all the fun he gets out of that pony. I want to again remind you to write to Georgio Rambottom or to his boss to fix up that wall to the little garden that madame Isotta uses, for it is all flat on the ground now as I have already told him a lot of times, for all the good that does, so I am writing to your lordship in the matter I have done all that I can, for all the good that does as noboddy hear can do anything without you.

     your faithful

         LUNARDA DA PALLA.
         20 Dec. 1454."

". . . gone over it with all the foremen and engineers. And about the silver for the small medal . . ."

"*Magnifice ac potens . . .*
        because the walls of . . ."

"*Malatesta de Malatestis ad Magnificum Dominum Patremque suum.*

"Ex^{so} D^{no} et D^{no} sin D^{no} Sigismundum Pandolfi Filium
        Malatestis Capitan General

Magnificent and Exalted Lord and Father in especial my lord with due recommendation: your letter has been presented to me by Gentilino da Gradara and with it the bay pony (ronzino baiectino) the which you have sent me, and which appears in my eyes a fine caparison'd charger, upon which I intend to learn all there is to know about riding, in consideration of yr. paternal affection for which I thank your excellency thus briefly and pray you continue to hold me in this esteem notifying you by the bearer of this that we are all in good health, as I hope and desire your Ex^{et} Lordship is also: with continued remembrance I remain
        Your son and servant
        MALATESTA DE MALATESTIS.
        Given in Rimini, this the 22nd day of December
        anno domini 1454"
        (*in the sixth year of his age*)

"ILLUSTRIOUS PRINCE:
    Unfitting as it is that I should offer counsels to Hannibal . . ."

"*Magnifice ac potens domine, domine mi singularissime, humili recomendatione premissa* etc. This to advise your M^{gt} Ld^{shp} how the second load of Veronese marble has finally got here, after being held up at Ferrara with no end of fuss and botheration, the whole of it having been there unloaded.

I learned how it happened, and it has cost a few florins to get back the said load which had been seized for the skipper's debt and defalcation; he having fled when the lighter was seized. But that Y^r M^{gt} Ld^{shp} may not lose the moneys paid out on his account I have had the lighter brought here and am holding it, against his arrival. If not we still have the lighter.

As soon as the Xmas fêtes are over I will have the stone floor laid in the sacristy, for which the stone is already cut. The wall of the building is finished and I shall now get the roof on.

We have not begun putting new stone into the martyr chapel; first because the heavy frosts wd. certainly spoil the job; secondly because the aliofants aren't yet here and one can't get the measurements for the cornice to the columns that are to rest on the aliofants.

They are doing the stairs to your room in the castle . . . I have had Messire Antonio degli Atti's court paved and the stone benches put in it.

Ottavian is illuminating the bull. I mean the bull for the chapel. All the stone-cutters are waiting for spring weather to start work again.

The tomb is all done except part of the lid, and as soon as Messire Agostino gets back from Cesena I will see that he finishes it, ever recommending me to Y^r M^{gt} Ld^{shp}

believe me y^r faithful
PETRUS GENARIIS."

That's what they found in the post-bag
And some more of it to the effect that
he "lived and ruled"

"et amava perdutamente Ixotta degli Atti"
e *"ne fu degna"*
>   *"constans in proposito*
Placuit oculis principis
pulchra aspectu"
"populo grata (Italiaeque decus)"
"and built a temple so full of pagan works"
>   i. e. Sigismund
and in the style "Past ruin'd Latium"
The filigree hiding the gothic,
>   with a touch of rhetoric in the whole
And the old sarcophagi,
>   such as lie, smothered in grass, by San Vitale.

CANTO XIII

Kung walked
            by the dynastic temple
And into the cedar grove,
            and then out by the lower river,
And with him Khieu, Tchi
            and Tian the low speaking
And "we are unknown," said Kung,
"You will take up charioteering?
            Then you will become known,
Or perhaps I should take up charioteering, or archery?
Or the practice of public speaking?"
And Tseu-lou said, "I would put the defences in order,"
And Khieu said, "If I were lord of a province
I would put it in better order than this is."
And Tchi said, "I would prefer a small mountain temple,
With order in the observances,
            with a suitable performance of the ritual,"
And Tian said, with his hand on the strings of his lute
The low sounds continuing
            after his hand left the strings,
And the sound went up like smoke, under the leaves,
And he looked after the sound:
            "The old swimming hole,
And the boys flopping off the planks,
Or sitting in the underbrush playing mandolins."
            And Kung smiled upon all of them equally.

And Thseng-sie desired to know:
        "Which had answered correctly?"
And Kung said, "They have all answered correctly,
That is to say, each in his nature."
And Kung raised his cane against Yuan Jang,
        Yuan Jang being his elder,
For Yuan Jang sat by the roadside pretending
        to be receiving wisdom.
And Kung said
        "You old fool, come out of it,
Get up and do something useful."
        And Kung said
"Respect a child's faculties
From the moment it inhales the clear air,
But a man of fifty who knows nothing
        Is worthy of no respect."
And "When the prince has gathered about him
All the savants and artists, his riches will be fully employed."
And Kung said, and wrote on the bo leaves:
        If a man have not order within him
He can not spread order about him;
And if a man have not order within him
His family will not act with due order;
        And if the prince have not order within him
He can not put order in his dominions.
And Kung gave the words "order"
And "brotherly deference"
And said nothing of the "life after death."
And he said
        "Anyone can run to excesses,

21

It is easy to shoot past the mark,
It is hard to stand firm in the middle."

And they said: If a man commit murder
            Should his father protect him, and hide him?
And Kung said:
            He should hide him.

And Kung gave his daughter to Kong-Tch'ang
            although Kong-Tch'ang was in prison.
And he gave his niece to Nan-Young
            although Nan-Young was out of office.
And Kung said "Wang ruled with moderation,
            In his day the State was well kept,
And even I can remember
A day when the historians left blanks in their writings,
I mean for things they didn't know,
But that time seems to be passing."
A day when the historians left blanks in their writings,
But that time seems to be passing.
And Kung said, "Without character you will
            be unable to play on that instrument
Or to execute the music fit for the Odes.
The blossoms of the apricot
            blow from the east to the west,
And I have tried to keep them from falling."

CANTO XIV

Io venni in luogo d'ogni luce muto;
The stench of wet coal, politicians
. . . . e and . . . . .n, their, wrists bound to their ankles,
Standing bare bum,
Faces smeared on their rumps,
        wide eye on flat buttock,
Bush hanging for beard,
      Addressing crowds through their arse-holes,
Addressing the multitudes in the ooze,
       newts, water-slugs, water-maggots,
And with them . . . . r,
       a scrupulously clean table-napkin
Tucked under his penis,
       and . . . . m
Who disliked colloquial language,
Stiff-starched, but soiled, collars
       circumscribing his legs.
The pimply and hairy skin
       pushing over the collar's edge,
Profiteers drinking blood sweetened with shit,
And behind them . . . . . . f and the financiers
       lashing them with steel wires.

And the betrayers of language
      . . . . . . n and the press gang
And those who had lied for hire;
the perverts, the perverters of language,

                    the perverts, who have set money-lust
Before the pleasures of the senses;
howling, as of a hen-yard in a printing-house,
                    the clatter of presses,
the blowing of dry dust and stray paper,
fœtor, sweat, the stench of stale oranges,
dung, last cesspool of the universe,
mysterium, acid of sulphur,
the pusillanimous, raging;
plunging jewels in mud,
                    and howling to find them unstained;
sadic mothers driving their daughters to bed with decrepitude,
sows eating their litters,
and here the placard ΕΙΚΩΝ ΓΗΣ,
                    and here: THE PERSONNEL CHANGES,

melting like dirty wax,
                    decayed candles, the bums sinking lower,
faces submerged under hams,
And in the ooze under them,
reversed, foot-palm to foot-palm,
                    hand-palm to hand-palm, the agents provocateurs
The murderers of Pearse and Macdonagh,
                    Captain H. the chief torturer;
The petrified turd that was Verres,
                    bigots, Calvin and St. Clement of Alexandria!
black-beetles, burrowing into the shit,
The soil a decrepitude, the ooze full of morsels,
lost contours, erosions.
                    Above the hell-rot

the great arse-hole,
       broken with piles,
hanging stalactites,
       greasy as sky over Westminster,
the invisible, many English,
       the place lacking in interest,
last squalor, utter decrepitude,
the vice-crusaders, farting through silk,
       waving the Christian symbols,
. . . . frigging a tin penny whistle,
Flies carrying news, harpies dripping shit through the air,

The slough of unamiable liars,
       bog of stupidities,
malevolent stupidities, and stupidities,
the soil living pus, full of vermin,
dead maggots begetting live maggots,
       slum owners,
usurers squeezing crab lice, pandars to authority,
pets-de-loup, sitting on piles of stone books,
obscuring the texts with philology,
       hiding them under their persons,
the air without refuge of silence,
       the drift of lice, teething,
and above it the mouthing of orators,
       the arse-belching of preachers.
       And Invidia,
the corruptio, fœtor, fungus,
liquid animals, melted ossifications,

Slow rot, fœtid combustion,
        chewed cigar-butts, without dignity, without tragedy,
. . . . . m Episcopus, waving a condom full of black-beetles,
monopolists, obstructors of knowledge,
        obstructors of distribution.

And before hell mouth; dry plain
       and two mountains;
On the one mountain, a running form,
       and another
In the turn of the hill; in hard steel
The road like a slow screw's thread,
The angle almost imperceptible,
       so that the circuit seemed hardly to rise;
And the running form, naked, Blake,
Shouting, whirling his arms, the swift limbs,
Howling against the evil,
       his eyes rolling,
Whirling like flaming cartwheels,
       and his head held backward to gaze on the evil
As he ran from it,
       to be hid by the steel mountain,
And when he showed again from the north side;
       his eyes blazing toward hell mouth,
His neck forward,
       and like him Peire Cardinal.
And in the west mountain, Il Fiorentino,
Seeing hell in his mirror,
       and lo Sordels
Looking on it in his shield;
And Augustine, gazing toward the invisible.

And past them, the criminal
            lying in blue lakes of acid,
The road between the two hills, upward
            slowly,
The flames patterned in lacquer, crimen est actio,
The limbo of chopped ice and sawdust,
And I bathed myself with the acid to free myself
            of the hell ticks,
Scales, fallen louse eggs.
            Palux Laerna,
the lake of bodies, aqua morta,
of limbs fluid, and mingled, liked fish heaped in a bin,
and here an arm upward, clutching a fragment of marble,
And the embryos, in flux,
            new inflow, submerging,
Here an arm upward, trout, submerged by the eels;
            and from the bank, the stiff herbage
the dry nobbled path, saw many known, and unknown,
for an instant;
            submerging,
The face gone, generation.
            Then light air, under saplings,
the blue banded lake under æther,
            an oasis, the stones, the calm field,
the grass quiet,
            and passing the tree of the bough
The grey stone posts,
            and the stair of gray stone,
the passage clean-squared in granite:
            descending,

and I through this, and into the earth,
         patet terra,
entered the quiet air
         the new sky,
the light as after a sunset,
         and by their fountains, the heroes,
Sigismundo, and Malatesta Novello,
         and founders, gazing at the mounts of their cities.

The plain, distance, and in fount-pools
         the nymphs of that water
rising, spreading their garlands,
         weaving their water reeds with the boughs,
In the quiet,
         and now one man rose from his fountain
and went off into the plain.

Prone in that grass, in sleep;
         et j'entendis des voix: . . .

                          wall . . . Strasbourg
Galliffet led that triple charge . . . Prussians
  [Plarr's narration]
and he said
         it was for the honour of the army.
And they called him a swashbuckler.
         I didn't know what it was
But I thought: This is pretty bloody damn fine.
And my old nurse, he was a man nurse, and
He killed a Prussian and he lay in the street
there in front of our house for three days

And he stank . . . .
　　　Brother Percy,
And our Brother Percy . . .
　　　old Admiral
He was a middy in those days,
And they came into Ragusa
. . . . . . place those men went for the Silk War . . . . .
And they saw a procession coming down through
A cut in the hills, carrying something
The six chaps in front carrying a long thing
　　　　　on their shoulders,
And they thought it was a funeral,
　　　　　but the thing was wrapped up in scarlet,
And he put off in the cutter,
　　　　　he was a middy in those days,
To see what the natives were doing,
And they got up to the six fellows in livery,
And they looked at it, and I can still hear the old admiral,
"Was it? it was
　　　Lord Byron
Dead drunk, with the face of an a y n . . . . "
He pulled it out long, like that:
　　　　　"the face of an a y n . . . . gel."

And because that son of a bitch,
　　　　　Franz Josef of Austria . . . . . .
And because that son of a bitch Napoléon Barbiche . . .
They put Aldington on Hill 70, in a trench
　　　　　dug through corpses
With a lot of kids of sixteen,

Howling and crying for their mamas,
And he sent a chit back to his major:
                    I can hold out for ten minutes
With my sergeant and a machine gun.
                    And they rebuked him for levity.
And Henri Gaudier went to it,
                    and they killed him,
And killed a good deal of sculpture,
And ole T.E.H. he went to it,
With a lot of books from the library,
London Library, and a shell buried 'em in a dugout,
And the Library expressed its annoyance.
                    And a bullet hit him on the elbow
... gone through the fellow in front of him,
And he read Kant in the hospital, in Wimbledon,
in the original,
And the hospital staff didn't like it.

And Wyndham Lewis went to it,
With a heavy bit of artillery,
                    and the airmen came by with a mitrailleuse,
And cleaned out most of his company,
                    and a shell lit on his tin hut,
While he was out in the privy,
                    and he was all there was left of that outfit.

Windeler went to it,
                    and he was out in the Ægæan,
And down in the hold of his ship
                    pumping gas into a sausage,

And the boatswain looked over the rail,
          down into amidships, and he said:
          Gees! look a' the Kept'n,
The Kept'n's a-gettin' 'er up.

And Ole Captain Baker went to it,
          with his legs full of rheumatics,
So much so he couldn't run,
          so he was six months in hospital,
Observing the mentality of the patients.

And Fletcher was 19 when he went to it,
And his major went mad in the control pit,
          about midnight, and started throwing the 'phone about
And he had to keep him quiet
          till about six in the morning,
And direct that bunch of artillery.

And Ernie Hemingway went to it,
          too much in a hurry,
And they buried him for four days.

Et ma foi, vous savez,
          tous les nerveux. Non,
Y a une limite; les bêtes, les bêtes ne sont
Pas faites pour ça, c'est peu de chose un cheval.
Les hommes de 34 ans à quatre pattes
          qui criaient "maman." Mais les costauds,
La fin, là à Verdun, n'y avait que ces gros bonshommes
          Et y voyaient extrêmement clair.

Qu'est-ce que ça vaut, les généraux, le lieutenant,
on les pèse à un centigramme,
            n'y a rien que du bois,
Notr' capitaine, tout, tout ce qu'il y a de plus renfermé
            de vieux polytechnicien, mais solide,
La tête solide. Là, vous savez,
Tout, tout fonctionne, et les voleurs, tous les vices,
Mais les rapaces,
            y avait trois dans notre compagnie, tous tués.
Y sortaient fouiller un cadavre, pour rien,
            y n'seraient sortis pour rien que ça.
Et les boches, tout ce que vous voulez,
            militarisme, et cætera, et cætera.
Tout ça, mais, MAIS,
            l'français, i s'bat quand y a mangé.
Mais ces pauvres types
A la fin y s'attaquaient pour manger,
            Sans ordres, les bêtes sauvages, on y fait
Prisonniers; ceux qui parlaient français disaient:
            "Poo quah? Ma foi on attaquait pour manger."

C'est le corr-ggras, le corps gras,
            leurs trains marchaient trois kilomètres à l'heure,
Et ça criait, ça grinçait, on l'entendait à cinq kilomètres.
(Ça qui finit la guerre.)

            Liste officielle des morts 5,000,000.

I vous dit, bè, voui, tout sentait le pétrole.
Mais, Non! je l'ai engueulé.
Je lui ai dit: T'es un con! T'a raté la guerre.

33

O voui! tous les hommes de goût, y conviens,
Tout ça en arrière.
                    Mais un mec comme toi!
C't homme, un type comme ça!
                    Ce qu'il aurait pu encaisser!
Il était dans une fabrique.
What, burying squad, terrassiers, avec leur tête
                    en arrière, qui regardaient comme ça,
On risquait la vie pour un coup de pelle,
Faut que ça soit bien carré, exact . . .

Dey vus a bolcheviki dere, und dey dease him:
Looka vat youah Trotzsk is done, e iss
                    madeh deh zhamefull beace!!
"He iss madeh deh zhamefull beace, iss he?
                    He is madeh de zhamevul beace?
A Brest-Litovsk, yess? Aint yuh herd?
                    He vinneh de vore.
De droobs iss released vrom de eastern vront, yess?
Un venn dey getts to deh vestern vront, iss it
                    How many getts dere?
And dose doat getts dere iss so full off revolutions
Venn deh vrench is come dhru, yess,
Dey say, 'Vot?' Un de posch say:
                    'Aint yeh heard? Say, ve got a rheffolution.'"

That's the trick with a crowd,
                    Get 'em into the street and get 'em moving.
And all the time, there were people going
Down there, over the river.

There was a man there talking,
To a thousand, just a short speech, and
Then move 'em on. And he said:
Yes, these people, they are all right, they
Can do everything, everything except act;
And go an' hear 'em, but when they are through,
      Come to the bolsheviki . . .

And when it broke, there was the crowd there,
And the cossacks, just as always before,
But one thing, the cossacks said:
      "Pojalouista."
And that got round in the crowd,
And then a lieutenant of infantry
Ordered 'em to fire into the crowd,
      in the square at the end of the Nevsky,
In front of the Moscow station,
And they wouldn't,
And he pulled his sword on a student for laughing,
And killed him,
And a cossack rode out of his squad
On the other side of the square
And cut down the lieutenant of infantry
And that was the revolution . . .
      as soon as they named it.

And you can't make 'em,
Nobody knew it was coming. They were all ready, the old gang,
Guns on the top of the post office and the palace,
But none of the leaders knew it was coming.

And there were some killed at the barracks,
But that was between the troops.

So we used to hear it at the opera,
That they wouldn't be under Haig;
       and that the advance was beginning;
That it was going to begin in a week.

Tempus loquendi
Tempus tacendi.
Said Mr Jefferson: It wd. have given us time.
"modern dress for your statue . . .
I remember having written you while Congress sat at Annapolis,
on water communication between ours and the western country,
particularly the information . . . of the plain between
Big Beaver and Cayohoga, which made me hope that a canal
. . . navigation of Lake Erie and the Ohio. You must have had
occasion of getting better information on this subject
and if you have you wd. oblige me
by a communication of it. I consider this canal,
if practicable, as a very important work."

                                        T. J. to General Washington, 1787.

. . . no slaves north of Maryland district . . .
. . . flower found in Connecticut that vegetates when suspended
        in air . . .
. . . screw more effectual if placed below surface of water.
Suspect that a countryman of ours, Mr Bushnell of Connecticut
is entitled to the merit of prior discovery.
Excellency Mr Adams. Excellency Dr Franklin.
And thus Mr Jefferson (president) to Tom Paine:
"You expressed a wish to get a passage to this country
in a public vessel. Mr Dawson is charged with orders
to the captain of the 'Maryland' to receive and accommodate you
with passage back, if you can depart on so short a warning . . .

in hopes you will find us returned to sentiments
worthy of former time . . . in these you have laboured as
much as any man living. That you may long live to
continue your labours and to reap their fitting reward . . .
Assurances of my high esteem and attachment."

"English papers . . . their lies . . ."

in a few years . . . no slaves northward of Maryland . . .

"Their tobacco, 9 millions, delivered in port of France;
6 millions to manufacture
on which the king takes thirty million
that cost 25 odd to collect
so that in all it costs 72 millions livres to the consumer . . .
persuaded (I am) in this branch of the revenue
the collection absorbs too much.

                              (from Paris, 1785)
. . . for our model, the Maison Quarrée of Nismes . . .

With respect to his motives (Madison writing) I acknowledged
I had been much puzzled to divine any natural ones
without looking deeper into human nature
than I was willing to do.

                        (in re Mr Robert Smith)
So critical the state of that country
moneyed men I imagine are glad to place their money abroad.
Mr Adams could borrow there for us.
This country is really supposed to be on the eve of a XTZBK49HT
                    (*parts of this letter in cypher*)

Jefferson, from Paris, to Madison, Aug. 2, 1787.
I hear that Mr Beaumarchais means to make himself heard . . .
. . . turn through the Potomac . . . commerce of Lake Erie . . .
I can further say with safety there is not a crowned head
in Europe whose talents or merits would entitle him
to be elected a vestryman by any American parish.
             T. J. to General Washington, May 2. '88.

"When Lafayette harangued you and me and John Quincy Adams
through a whole evening in your hotel in the Cul de Sac . . .
. . . silent as you were. I was, in plain truth as astonished
at the grossness of his ignorance of government and history,
as I had been for years before at that of Turgot,
La Rochefoucauld, of Condorcet and of Franklin."
        To Mr Jefferson, Mr John Adams.

. . . care of the letters now enclosed. Most of them are
of a complexion not proper for the eye of the police.
      From Monticello, April 16th. 1811
        To Mr Barlow departing for Paris.

. . . indebetd to nobody for more cordial aid than to Gallatin . . .

"Adair too had his kink. He believed all the Indians of
America to be descended from the jews."
        Mr Jefferson to Mr Adams.

"But observe that the public were at the same time paying
on it an interest of exactly the same amount
(four million dollars). Where then is the gain to either

party which makes it a public blessing?"
to Mr Eppes, 1813.

"Man, a rational creature!" said Franklin.
"Come, let us suppose a rational man.
Strip him of all his appetites, especially his hunger and thirst.
He is in his chamber, engaged in making experiments,
Or in pursuing some problem.
At this moment a servant knocks. 'Sir,
dinner is on the table.'
'Ham and chickens?' 'Ham!'
'And must I break the chain of my thoughts to
go down and gnaw a morsel of damned hog's arse?
Put aside your ham; I will dine tomorrow;'
Take away appetite, and the present generation would not
Live a month, and no future generation would exist;
and thus the exalted dignity of human nature etc. . . ."
Mr Adams to Mr Jefferson, 15 Nov. 1813.

". . . wish that I cd. subjoin Gosindi's Syntagma
of the doctrines of Epicurus."

(Mr Adams.)

". . . this was the state of things in 1785 . . ."

(Mr Jefferson.)

. . . met by agreement, about the close of the session —
Patrick Henry, Frank Lee and your father,
Henry Lee and myself . . . to consult . . . measures
circumstances of times seemed to call for . . .
produce some channel of correspondence . . . this was in '73.
Jefferson to D. Carr.

... church of St. Peter ... human reason, human conscience,
though I believe that there are such things ...

Mr Adams.

A tiel leis ... en ancien scripture, and this
they have translated *Holy Scripture* ...

Mr Jefferson.

and they continue this error.
"Bonaparte ... knowing nothing of commerce ...
... or paupers, who are about one fifth of the whole ...'"
   (on the state of England in 1814).

Hic Explicit Cantus

from CANTO XXXVIII

A factory
has also another aspect, which we call the financial aspect
It gives people the power to buy (wages, dividends
which are power to buy) but it is also the cause of prices
or values, financial, I mean financial values
It pays workers, and pays *for* material.
What it pays in wages and dividends
stays fluid, as power to buy, and this power is less,
per forza, damn blast your intellex, is less
than the total payments made by the factory
(as wages, dividends AND payments for raw material
bank charges etcetera,
and all, that is the whole, that is the total
of these is added into the total of prices
caused by that factory, any damn factory
and there is and must be therefore a clog
and the power to purchase can never
(under the present system) catch up with
prices at large,

       and the light became so bright and so blindin'
in this layer of paradise
      that the mind of man was bewildered.

from CANTO XLII

Fixed in the soul, nell'anima, of the Illustrious College
They had been ten years proposing such a Monte,
That is a species of bank — damn good bank, in Siena

A mount, a bank, a fund, a bottom, an
institution of credit.
a place to send cheques in and out of
and yet not yet a banco di giro, and the Bailey
sought views from the Senate "With paternal affection
justice convenience of city what college had with such
foresight wherefore S. A. (Your Highness) as in register
Nov. 1624
following details: as third, a Yearly balance
as 5th that any citizen shall have right to deposit
and to fruits therefrom resultant at five percent annual interest
and that borrowers pay a bit over that
for services (dei ministri) that is for running expenses
and book keeping which shall be counted a half scudo
per hundred per year
(All of this is important)
and 6thly that the Magistrate
give his chief care that the specie
be lent to whomso can best use it USE IT
(*id est, più utilmente*)
to the good of their houses, to benefit of their business
as of weaving, the wool trade, the silk trade
And that (7thly) the overabundance every five years shall the Bailey

distribute to workers of the contrade (the wards) holding in
reserve a prudent proportion as against unforseen losses
though there shd. be NO such losses
and 9th that the borrowers can pay up before the end of their term
whenso it be to their interest. No debt to run more than five years.
July 1623
Loco Signi
X [a cross in the margin]
That profit on deposits should be used to cover all losses and the
distributions of the fifth year be made from remaining profits, after
restoration of losses no (*benché*) matter how small
with sane small reserve against future idem
I, Livio Pasquini, notary, citizen of Siena, most faithfully copied
July 18th. 1623
Consules, Iudices, and notary public pro serenissimo
attest Livio's superscript next date being November,

> wave falls and the hand falls

Thou shalt not always walk in the sun

> or see weed sprout over cornice

Thy work in set space of years, not over an hundred.

That the Mount of Pity (or Hock Shop)
municipal of Siena has lent only on pledges
that is on stuff actually hocked . . . wd be we believe useful
and beneficent that there be place to lend licitly
MONEY to receive licitly money
at moderate and legitimate interest
was sent months ago to YYour HHighness AA VV a memorial
to erect a New Mountain
could accept specie from Universities (id est congregations)

and individuals and from Luoghi
i. e. companies and persons both public and private
WHOMSOEVER

not requiring that they have special privilege
because of their state or conditions but to folk of
ANY CONDITION
         that the same Mount cd/lend on good Mallevadoria
(that is security) at the same rate plus a little over
to cover current expenses of supervisors and employees
& being sent to YY. HHighnesses (AA. VV. = YY HH)
that you might understand it
that it be brought to consideration with certain details
discussed first orally and then put into writing
(in what wd. seem to have been 1622)
Stating that Siena had no income and Their Highnesses
had provided credit from customs
and from miscellaneous taxes
and that the Grand Duke hadn't lost anything by it
Plus a list of Sienese assets (coolish)
Plus a lien on "The Abundance"
And knowing that all this is but a little
Pledge the persons and goods of the laity
And leave open door to other towns in the state
who care to give similar pledges
And that whoso puts in money shall have lots in the Monte
that yield 5% interest
and that these shareholders shall receive their due fruit
And that the Gd. Duke make known at Siena
to the same deputies of the Bailey . . .
but that it be separate from the Pawn Shop

and have its own magistrates and employees
and that YYour HHighnesses send approbation
commanding their will, we humbly with reverence
... the 29th day of Xember 1622 ...

       servants of YYour HHighnesses

                         Nicolo de Antille
                         Horatio Gionfiglioli
                         Sebastiano Cellesi

       TTheir HHighnesses gratified
       the city of this demand to
       erect a New Monte
       for good public and private and to facilitate ...
       ... agreed to accommodate
       ... and to lend the fund against the Gd. Duke's
       public entries to the sum of
       200,000 scudi
       capital for fruit at 5% annual
       which is 10,000 a year
       assigned on the office of grazing
       on caution of said security offered
       leaving ground for other towns that
       wish to participate

               with TTheir HHighnesses
               approbations as follows:

Maria Maddalena Tutrice

        Horº della Rena 30 Xembre 1622

Needs a stamp
refer to
the Governor

Fabbizio bollo
   vedo
Governatore   the illustrious Bailey
executed in toto & as per true rescript of
                        TTheir HHighnesses
   2 Jan 1622
                  Cenzio Grcolini
which date goes in the Sienese calendar
whereof December was the x th month and
             March was the New Year
                  ACTUM SENIS, the
Parish of San Joannij in the Gd. Ducal Palace
present the Marquis Joanne Christophoro   the
illustrious Marquis Antony Mary of Malaspina
and the most renowned Johnny something or other de Binis
Florentine Senator, witness and I notary undersigned
Ego Livius Pasquinus of Marius
(deceased) filius Apostolic Imperial and Pontifical notary
public Judge Ordinary, Citizen of Siena
WHEREFORE
         let all sundry and whoever be
satisfied that the said MOUNT may be created,
so that the echo turned back in my mind: Pavia.
Saw cities move in one figure, Vicenza, as depicted,
San Zeno by Adige . . .
          I Nicolaus Ulivis
de Cagnascis citizen of Pistoja Florentine notary public
countersigning
          Senatus Populusque Senensis

ob pecuniae scarcitatem
                    borrowing, rigging exchanges,
licit consumption impeded
                    and it is getting steadily WORSE
others with specie abundant do not use it in business
(to be young is to suffer.
            Be old, and be past that)
do not use it in business and everyone remains here
without work
few come to buy in the market
                    fewer still work the fields
Monte non vacabilis publico
shares not to expire with death . . . will TTheir HHighnesses
against public entries
get that straight — capital two hundred thousand
which wd. correspond to 10,000 income
on the entries of the office of grazing
with precautions (cauteles)
to guarantee their same Highnesses against any possible loss
Which idea dates at least to July 1623
die decima ottava
and other copies 1624, 1622
which seems to have been approved "last October"
by Della Rena and M. Magdalene the She Guardian,
tutrice, more or less regent
Don Ferdinandus Secundus Dux Magnus
and his Serenest she-tutrices
with public documentation
for public and private utility
foreseeing erection

legitimate and just, such a MOUNTAIN

Chigi, Soffici, Marcellus de? Illuri,
no, Marcellus Austini, Caloanes Marescotti and
Lord Mt Alban effected
that the officers of this Mountain
and in time to come all their successors
shares that shall be called Loca Montis —
Have you a place on the Hill, sir?
                out of sure knowledge and
ex certe scientia et in plenitude of their powers
inviolable for observance, so to be comprehended
10 thousand scudi
de libris septeno
? one scudo worth 7 lire
in respect to 200,000 (two hundred thousand).

to the end:
>   four fat oxen
having their arses wiped
and in general being tidied up to serve god under my window
with stoles of Imperial purple
with tassels, and grooms before the carroccio
on which carroch six lion heads
>   to receive the wax offering
Thus arrive the gold eagles, the banners of the contrade,
and boxes of candles
>   "Mn-YaWWH!!!"
Said the left front ox, suddenly,
"pnAWH!" as they tied on his red front band,
St George, two hokey-pokey stands and the unicorn
>   "Nicchio! Nicch-iO-né!!"
The kallipygous Sienese females
get that way from the *salite*
>   that is from continual plugging up hill
One box marked "200 LIRE"
>   "laudate pueri"
alias serve God with candles
with the palio and 17 banners
and when six men had hoisted up the big candle
a bit askew in the carroch and the fore ox had
been finally arse-wiped
they set off toward the Duomo, time
consumed 1 hour and 17 minutes.

And thou shalt not, Firenze 1766, and thou shalt not
sequestrate for debt any farm implement
nor any yoke ox nor
any peasant while he works with the same.
                    Pietro Leopoldo
Heavy grain crop unsold
never had the Mount lacked for specie, cut rate to four and ⅓ rd

creditors had always been paid,
that trade inside the Grand Duchy be free of impediments
shut down on grain imports
'83, four percent legal maximum interest
'85, three on church investments, motu proprio
Pietro Leopoldo
Ferdinando EVVIVA!!
                    declared against exportation
thought grain was to eat

Flags trumpets horns drums
and a placard
                VIVA FERDINANDO
and were sounded all carillons
with bombs and with bonfires and was sung TE DEUM
in thanks to the Highest for this so
provident law
and were lights lit in the chapel of Alexander
        and the image of the Madonna unveiled

and sung litanies and then went to St Catherine's chapel
in S. Domenico and by the reliquary
of the Saint's head sang prayers and
went to the Company Fonte Giusta
also singing the litanies
and when was this thanksgiving ended the cortege
and the contrade with horns drums
trumpets and banners went to the
houses of the various ambulant vendors, then were the sticks of the
flags set in the stanchions on the Palace of the Seignors
and the gilded placard between them
(thus ended the morning)
        meaning to start in the afternoon
and the big bell and all bells of the tower in the piazza
sounded from 8 a. m. until seven o'clock in the evening
without intermission and next day was procession
coaches and masks in great number
and of every description e di tutte le qualità
    to the sound always of drums and trumpets
crying VIVA FERDINANDO and in all parts of the piazza
were flames in great number and grenades burning
to sound of bombs and of mortaretti and the shooting of
guns and of pistols and in chapel of the Piazza
a great number of candles for the publication of this so
provident law and at sundown were dances
    and the masks went into their houses
and the captains of the ward companies,
the contrade, took their banners to the Piazza chapel
where once more they sang litanies
and cried again Ferdinando EVVIVA

Evviva Ferdinando il Terzo
and from the contrade continued the drumming
and blowing of trumpets and hunting horns,
torch flares, grenades and they went to the Piazza del Duomo
with a new hullabaloo gun shots mortaretti and pistols
there were no streets not ablaze with the torches
or with wood fires and straw flares
and the vendors had been warned not to show goods for
        fear of disorder and stayed all that day withindoors
or else outside Siena. This was a law called
Dovizia annonaria
                    to be freed from the Yoke of Licence
From October 9th until the 3rd of November
was unforeseen jubilation, four lines of tablet in marble:
                    Frumentorum licentia
            coercita de annonaria laxata Pauperum aeque
                    divitium bono conservit
            FERDINANDI 1792
refused to take with him objects of small bulk which he
held to be the property of the nation. Ferd III. 1796
that the sovereign be il più galantuomo del paese

the citizen priest Fr Lenzini mounted the tribune
to join the citizen Abrâm
and in admiring calm sat there with them the citizen
the Archbishop
                    from 7,50 a bushel to 12
        by the 26th April

and on June 28th came men of Arezzo
past the Porta Romana and went into the ghetto

there to sack and burn hebrews
part were burned with the liberty tree in the piazza
and for the rest of that day and night
1799 anno domini
Pillage stopped by superior order 3rd July was discovered a treason
in the cartridges given the troops
that is were full of semolina, not powder
        and cherry stone where shd/have been ball
and in others too little powder
Respectons les prêtres, remarked Talleyrand
1800 a good grain and wine year
            if you wd/get on well with the peasantry
of the peninsula.
                    Premier Brumaire:
Vous voudrez citoyen
turn over all sums in yr / cash box
to the community, fraternité, greetings.
                            Delort
acting for Dupont Lieutenant General
Louis King of Etruria, Primus, absolute, without constitution.
Taxes so heavy that are thought to be more than
paid by subjects of Britain.
                Gen. Clarke to the Ministro degli Esteri
Whereas the fruits of the Mount were the 2/3rds of the one percent
wherewith to pay all current expenses. Madame ma soeur et cousine
I have received Your Majesty's letter of
November twenty-fourth I
suppose that in the actual circumstances
She will be in a hurry to get to Spain or at least to
leave a country where she can no longer

stay with the dignity befitting her rank.
I have given orders that she be
received in my kingdom of Italy
and in my French States with honours that are due her.
If your Majesty should be in Milan or Turin
before the 18th of december I should have the
advantage of seeing her. I am sending an officer my
aide de camp, General Reile who will deliver this letter.
He will be charged at the same time to take measures
for the security of the country and
to remove men who could trouble its quiet,
        since I learn that Your Majesty has already thought necessary
to import troops from Lisbon.
My troops shd have by now entered that capital
and taken possession of Portugal
Wherewith I pray God, Madam my sister and cousin,
he be pleased to have you in holy and worthy keeping

At Venice, december fifth 1807
            Your Majesty's kind brother and cousin
                    NAPOLEON
(his secretary mixing the pronouns
"You," "She," "she" all to Majesty)
And those men who "with bestial enthusiasm" took horse place
were, says the much lesser Bandini, paid by the prefect
and beforehand prepared.

"Artists high rank, in fact sole social summits
which the tempest of politics can not reach,"
        which remark appears to have been made by
                                Napoleon

And "Semiramis" 1814 departed from Lucca
    but her brother's law code remains,
monumento di civile sapienza —
dried swamps, grew cotton, brought in merinos
mortgage system improved —
        "Thank god such men be but few"
though they build up human courage.
And before him had been Pietro Leopoldo
who wished state debt brought to an end;
who put the guilds under common tribunal;
who left names only as "vestige of feudal chain";
who lightened mortmain that princes and church be under tax
as were others; who ended the gaolings for debt;
who said thou shalt not sell public offices;
who suppressed so many *gabelle*;
who freed the printers of surveillance
        and wiped out the crime of lèse majesty;
who abolished death as a penalty and all tortures in prisons
which he held were for segregation;
who split common property among tillers;
roads, trees, and the wool trade,
the silk trade, and a set price, lower, for salt;
plus another full page of such actions Habsburg Lorraine
His son the Third Ferdinando, cut taxes by half,
improved tillage in Val di Chiana, Livorno porto franco.

        and this day came Madame Letizia,
the ex-emperor's mother, and on the 13th departed.

"The foundation, Siena, has been to keep bridle on usury."
    Nicolò Piccolomini, Provveditore.

CANTO XLV

With *Usura*

With usura hath no man a house of good stone
each block cut smooth and well fitting
that design might cover their face,
with usura
hath no man a painted paradise on his church wall
harpes et luz
or where virgin receiveth message
and halo projects from incision,
with usura
seeth no man Gonzaga his heirs and his concubines
no picture is made to endure nor to live with
but it is made to sell and sell quickly
with usura, sin against nature,
is thy bread ever more of stale rags
is thy bread dry as paper,
with no mountain wheat, no strong flour
with usura the line grows thick
with usura is no clear demarcation
and no man can find site for his dwelling.
Stone-cutter is kept from his stone
weaver is kept from his loom
WITH USURA
wool comes not to market
sheep bringeth no gain with usura
Usura is a murrain, usura

blunteth the needle in the maid's hand
and stoppeth the spinner's cunning. Pietro Lombardo
came not by usura
Duccio came not by usura
nor Pier della Francesca; Zuan Bellin' not by usura
nor was "La Calunnia" painted.
Came not by usura Angelico; came not Ambrogio Praedis,
Came no church of cut stone signed: *Adamo me fecit.*
Not by usura St Trophime
Not by usura Saint Hilaire,
Usura rusteth the chisel
It rusteth the craft and the craftsman
It gnaweth the thread in the loom
None learneth to weave gold in her pattern;
Azure hath a canker by usura; cramoisi is unbroidered
Emerald findeth no Memling
Usura slayeth the child in the womb
It stayeth the young man's courting
It hath brought palsey to bed, lyeth
between the young bride and her bridegroom

CONTRA NATURAM

They have brought whores for Eleusis
Corpses are set to banquet
at behest of usura.

USURY: *A charge for the use of purchasing power, levied without regard to production; often without regard to the possibilities of production. (Hence the failure of the Medici bank.)*

Know then:
>   Toward summer when the sun is in Hyades
Sovran is Lord of the Fire
>   to this month are birds
With bitter smell and with the odour of burning
to the hearth god, lungs of the victim
>   The green frog lifts up his voice
>   and the white latex is in flower
In red car with jewels incarnadine
>   to welcome the summer
In this month no destruction
>   no tree shall be cut at this time
Wild beasts are driven from field
>   in this month are simples gathered.
The empress offers cocoons to the Son of Heaven
>   Then goes the sun into Gemini
Virgo in mid heaven at sunset
>   indigo must not be cut
No wood burnt into charcoal
>   gates are all open, no tax on the booths.
Now mares go to grazing,
>   tie up the stallions
Post up the horsebreeding notices
>   Month of the longest days
Life and death are now equal
>   Strife is between light and darkness
Wise man stays in his house

Stag droppeth antlers
Grasshopper is loud,
            leave no fire open to southward.
Now the sun enters Hydra, this is the third moon of summer
Antares of Scorpio stands mid heaven at sunset
Andromeda is with sunrise
            Lord of the fire is dominant
To this month is SEVEN,
            with bitter smell, with odour of burning
Offer to gods of the hearth
            the lungs of the victims
Warm wind is rising, cricket bideth in wall
Young goshawk is learning his labour
            dead grass breedeth glow-worms.
In Ming T'ang HE bideth
            in the west wing of that house
Red car and the sorrel horses
            his banner incarnadine.
The fish ward now goes against crocodiles
To take all great lizards, turtles, for divination,
sea terrapin.
The lake warden to gather rushes
            to take grain for the *manes*
to take grain for the beasts you will sacrifice
to the Lords of the Mountains
            To the Lords of great rivers
Inspector of dye-works, inspector of colour and broideries
see that the white, black, green be in order
let no false colour exist here
black, yellow, green be of quality

This month are trees in full sap
Rain has now drenched all the earth
            dead weeds enrich it, as if boil'd in a bouillon.
Sweet savour, the heart of the victim
yellow flag over Emperor's chariot
            yellow stones in his girdle.
Sagittarius in mid-course at sunset
            cold wind is beginning. Dew whitens.
Now is cicada's time,
        the sparrow hawk offers birds to the spirits.
Emperor goes out in war car, he is drawn by white horses,
white banner, white stones in his girdle
eats dog and the dish is deep.
            This month is the reign of Autumn
Heaven is active in metals, now gather millet
            and finish the flood-walls
Orion at sunrise.
        Horses now with black manes.
Eat dog meat. This is the month of ramparts.
Beans are the tribute, September is end of thunder
The hibernants go into their caves.
        Tolls lowered, now sparrows, they say, turn into oysters
The wolf now offers his sacrifice.
            Men hunt with five weapons,
They cut wood for charcoal.
        New rice with your dog meat.
First month of winter is now
        sun is in Scorpio's tail
at sunrise in Hydra, ice starting
The pheasant plunges into Hoai (great water)

61

and turns to an oyster
Rainbow is hidden awhile.
Heaven's Son feeds on roast pork and millet,
Steel gray are stallions.
This month winter ruleth.
The sun is in archer's shoulder
in crow's head at sunrise
Ice thickens. Earth cracks. And the tigers now move to mating.
Cut trees at solstice, and arrow shafts of bamboo.
Third month, wild geese go north,
magpie starts building,
Pheasant lifteth his voice to the Spirit of Mountains
The fishing season is open,
rivers and lakes frozen deep
Put now ice in your ice-house,
the great concert of winds
Call things by the names. Good sovereign by distribution
Evil king is known by his imposts.
Begin where you are said Lord Palmerston,
began draining swamps in Sligo
Fought smoke nuisance in London. Dredged harbour in Sligo.

 *chih*³

CANTO LIII

Yeou taught men to break branches
Seu Gin set up the stage and taught barter,
              taught the knotting of cords
Fou Hi taught men to grow barley
              2837 ante Christum
and they know still where his tomb is
by the high cypress between the strong walls.
the FIVE grains, said Chin Nong, that are
              wheat, rice, millet, *gros blé* and chick peas
and made a plough that is used five thousand years
Moved his court then to Kio-feou-hien
held market at mid-day
"bring what we have not here," wrote an herbal
Souan yen bagged fifteen tigers
              made signs out of bird tracks
Hoang Ti contrived the making of bricks
and his wife started working the silk worms,
              money was in days of Hoang Ti.
He measured the length of Syrinx
              of the tubes to make tune for song
Twenty-six (that was) eleven ante Christum
              had four wives and 25 males of his making
His tomb is today in Kiao-Chan
Ti Ko set his scholars to fitting words to their music
              is buried in Tung Kieou
This was in the twenty-fifth century a. C.
              YAO like the sun and rain,

saw what star is at solstice
saw what star marks mid summer
YU, leader of waters,

    black earth is fertile, wild silk still is from Shantung,
Ammassi, to the provinces,

    let his men pay tithes in kind.
"Siu-tcheou province to pay in earth of five colours,
Pheasant plumes from Yu-chan of mountains
Yu-chan to pay sycamores,

    of this wood are lutes made,
Ringing stones from Se-choui river
and grass that is called Tsing-mo" or μῶλυ,
Chun to the spirit Chang Ti, of heaven
moving the sun and stars

    que vos vers expriment vos intentions,
    et que la musique conforme

YAO

                       KAO-YAO

CHUN

YU

                      abundance.

Then an Empress fled with Chao Kang in her belly.
Fou-hi by virtue of wood;
Chin-nong, of fire; Hoang Ti ruled by the earth,
Chan by metal.
Tchuen was lord, as is water.
CHUN, govern
YU, cultivate,
The surface is not enough,
   from Chang Ti nothing is hidden.
For years no waters came, no rain fell
  for the Emperor Tching Tang,
grain scarce, prices rising
so that in 1760 Tching Tang opened the copper mine (ante Christum)
made discs with square holes in their middles
  and gave these to the people
wherewith they might buy grain
     where there was grain
The silos were emptied
7 years of sterility
   der im Baluba das Gewitter gemacht hat
Tching prayed on the mountain and
  wrote MAKE IT NEW
on his bathtub
  Day by day make it new
cut underbrush,
pile the logs
keep it growing.
Died Tching aged years an hundred,
in the 13th of his reign.

 hsin¹

 jih⁴

"We are up, Hia is down."
Immoderate love of women
Immoderate love of riches,
Cared for parades and huntin'.

jih⁴

Chang Ti above alone rules.
Tang not stinting of praise:

hsin¹

Consider their sweats, the people's
If you wd/ sit calm on the throne.

Hsia

Hia! Hia is fallen
for offence to the spirits,
For sweats of the people.
Not by your virtue
but by virtue of Tching Tang
Honour to YU, converter of waters
Honour Tching Tang
Honour to YIN
seek old men and new tools
After five hundred years came then Wen Wang
B. C. 1231
Uncle Ki said: Jewels!
You eat nothing but bears' paws.
In marble tower of Lou Tai doors were of jasper
that palace was ten years in the making
Tan Ki, palace, lit by day with torches and lanthorns
Now Kieou's daughter
was baked in an ox and served.
And they worked out the Y-king or changes

                    to guess from
In plain of Mou Ye, Cheou-sin came as a forest moving
          Wu Wang entered the city
gave out grain till the treasures were empty
by the Nine vases of YU, demobilized army
                    sent horses to Hoa-chan
                    To the peach groves
Dated his year from the winter solstice.
                    Red was his dynasty.
Kids 8 to 15 in the schools, then higher training
mottoes writ all over walls
                    "Use their ways and their music
                    Keep form of their charts and banners
                    Prepare soldiers in peace time
                    All is lost in the nightclubs
                        that was gained under good rule."
Wagon with small box wherein was a needle
                    that pointed to southward
and this was called the South Chariot.
          Lo Yang in the middle Kingdom and its length
was 17200 feet. Saith Tcheou Kong: True sage seeks not repose.
          Hope without work is crazy,
Your forebear among the people
                    dressed as one of the people
Caring for needs of the people,
                    old when he came to the throne
Observing the solstice.
          Died eleven o six ante Christum
                    are still bits of his writing
"A good governor is as wind over grass

A good ruler keeps down taxes."
Tching-ouang kept lynx eye on bureaucrats,
          lynx eye on the currency
weight of the tchu was one 24th of an ounce
          or one hundred grains of millet,
cloth bolt and silk bolt
to be two feet two inches by four tchang (one tchang equals four
    feet)
reigned till 1079
          and was peace for the rest of his reign.
Called for his hat shaped as a mortar board,
          set out the precious stones on his table
saying this is my will and my last will:
          Keep peace
Keep the peace, care for the people.
          Ten lines, no more in his testament.
Chao Kong called the historians,
          laid out white and violet damask
For the table of jewels, as when Tching-ouang received princes.
On the table of the throne of the West
          laid out the charters
constitutions of antient kings and two sorts of stone
Hong-pi and Yuen-yen,
And on the East table he put the pearls from Mt Hoa-chan
and pearls from the islands and the sphere of Chun
that showeth the places of heaven. And the dance robes of In
the old dynasty and the great drum that is 8 feet high
these he put in the place for music. The pikes, bows,
bamboo arrows and war gear he set to the East.
The mats of the first rank, of rushes bordered with damask

of the second of bamboo and the third rank,
of tree bark.
A gray fur cap for the crowning, and 20-ft halbards.
(Ten seven eight ante Christum)
"Left in my Father's orders, By the table of jewels
To administrate as in the law left us
        Keep peace in the Empire,
Ouen Ouang, and Wu Wang your fathers."
Thus came Kang to be Emperor/.
White horses with sorrel manes in the courtyard.
        "I am pro-Tcheou" said Confucius
        "I am" said Confutzius "pro-Tcheou in politics"
Wen-wang and Wu-wang had sage men, strong as bears
        Said young Kang-wang:
                Help me to keep the peace!
Your ancestors have come one by one under our rule
        for our rule,
Honour to Chao-Kong the surveyor.
        Let his name last 3000 years
Gave each man land for his labour
        not by plough-land alone
But for keeping of silk-worms
        Reforested the mulberry groves
        Set periodical markets
Exchange brought abundance, the prisons were empty.
"Yao and Chun have returned"
        sang the farmers
"Peace and abundance bring virtue." I am
        "pro-Tcheou" said Confucius five centuries later.
With his mind on this age.

Chou

In the 16th of Kang Ouang died Pé-kin
        Prince of Lou, friend of peace, friend of the people
          worthy son of Tcheou-kong
And in the 26th Kang Ouang, died Chao-Kong the tireless
      on a journey he made for good of the state
and men never thereafter cut branches
      of the pear-trees whereunder he had sat deeming justice
      deeming the measures of lands.
And you will hear to this day the folk singing
        Grow pear-boughs, be fearless
        let no man break twig of this tree
        that gave shade to Chao-Kong
        he had shadow from sun here;
          rest had he in your shade.
Died then Kang Wang in the 26th of his reign.   *b. c. 1053*
Moon shone in an haze of colours
Water boiled in the wells, and died Tchao-ouang
        to joy of the people.
Tchao-ouang that hunted across the tilled fields
And MOU-OUANG said:
        "as a tiger against me,
          a man of thin ice in thaw
aid me in the darkness of rule"
        then fell into vanity
against council led out a myriad army and brought back
4 wolves and 4 deer

70

his folk remained mere barbarians.
Yet when neared an hundred
         he wd/ have made reparation
Criminal law is from Chun,
         from necessity only
In doubt, no condemnation, rule out irrelevant evidence.
Law of MOU is law of the just middle, the pivot.
Riches that come of court fines and of judges' takings
         these are no treasure
as is said in the book *Lin hing* of the *Chu King*,
And the governor's daughters, three daughters,
came to the river King-Ho,
         For ten months was the emperor silent
and in the twelfth month, he, KONG, burnt the town
         and got over it
Song turned against Y-wang, great hail upon
         Hiao wang
killing the cattle, Han-kiang was frozen over.
And in this time was the horse dealer Fei-tsei
industrious, of the fallen house of Pe-y
who became master of equerry, who became Prince of Tsin.
Li WANG avid of silver, to whom a memorial
"A Prince who wd/ fulfill obligation, takes caution
à ce que l'argent circule"
         that cash move amongst the people.
"Glory of HEOU-TSIE is clouded
Deathless his honour that saw his folk using their substance.
The end of your house is upon us."
         Youi-leang-fou, in memorial.   *b.c. 860*
Said Chao-Kong: Talk of the people

is like the hills and the streams
thence comes our abundance.
To be Lord to the four seas of China
a man must let men make verses
he must let people play comedies
and historians write down the facts
he must let the poor speak evil of taxes.
Interregnum of Cong-ho. Siuen went against the west Tartars
His praise lasts to this day: Siuen-ouang contra barbaros
legat belli ducem Chaoumoukong,
Hoailand, fed by Hoai river,
dark millet, Tchang wine for the sacrifice.
Juxta fluvium Hoai acies ordinatur nec mora
Swift men as if flyers, like Yangtse
Strong as the Yangtse,
they stand rooted as mountains
they move as a torrent of waters
Emperor not rash in council: agit considerate
HAN founded the town of Yuei
and taught men to sow the five grains
In the 4th year of Siuen,
Sié was founded,
and there were four years of dry summer.
RITE is:
Nine days before the first moon of spring time,
that he fast. And with gold cup of wheat-wine
that he go afield to spring ploughing
that he plough one and three quarters furrows
and eat beef when this rite is finished,
so did not Siuen

that after famine, called back the people
>   where are reeds to weave, where are pine trees
Siuen established this people hac loca fluvius alluit
>   He heard the wild geese crying sorrow
Campestribus locis
>   here have we fixed our dwelling
>   after our sorrow,
our grandsons shall have our estate
The Lady Pao Sse brought earthquakes. TCHEOU falleth,
>   folly, folly, false fires no true alarm
>   Mount Ki-chan is broken.
Ki-chan is crumbled in the 10th moon of the 6th year of Yëou
>   Ouang
Sun darkened, the rivers were frozen . . .
>   and at this time was Tçin rising, a marquis on the
>   Tartar border
Empire down in the rise of princes
Tçin drave the Tartar, lands of the emperor idle
Tcheou tombs fallen in ruin
>   from that year was no order
No man was under another
>   9 Tcheou wd/ not stand together
>   were not rods in a bundle
Sky dark, cloudless and starless
>   at midnight a rain of stars
>   Wars,
>   wars without interest
boredom of an hundred years' wars.
>   And in Siang, the princes impatient
killed a bad king for a good one, and thus Ouen Kong

came to their rule in Sung land
            and they said Siang had been killed when hunting
Ouen cherished the people.
            States of Lou were unhappy
Their Richards poisoned young princes.
            All bloods, murders, all treasons —
Sons of the first wife of Ouen Kong.
Ling Kong loved to shoot from the hedges
        you'd see him behind a wall with his arrows
For fun of winging pedestrians
            this prince liked eating bears' paws.
By the Nine Urns of Yu, King Kong
made an alliance at hearing the sound of Tcheou music
This was the year of the two eclipses
        And Cheou-lang that held up the portcullis
        was named "hillock" because of a lump on his head
Man of Sung, and his line of Lou land
        and his second son was Kungfutseu
Taught and the not taught. Kung and Eleusis   仲   Chung
        to catechumen alone.
And when Kung was poor, a supervisor of victuals   尼   Ni
Pien's report boosted him
so that he was made supervisor of cattle
In that time were banquets as usual, Kung was inspector of markets
And that year was a comet in Scorpio
        and by night they fought in the boats on Kiang river
And King Wang thought to vary the currency
            μεταθεμένων τε τῶν χρωμένων
                        against council's opinion,
    and to gain by this wangling.

Honour to Fen-yang who resisted injustice,
And King Kong said "That idea is good doctrine
But I am too old to start using it."
Never were so many eclipses.
Then Kungfutseu was made minister and moved promptly against
    C. T. Mao
        and had him beheaded
that was false and crafty of heart
        a tough tongue that flowed with deceit
A man who remembered evil and was complacent in doing it.
LOU rose. Tsi sent girls to destroy it
        Kungfutseu retired
At Tching someone said:
            there is man with Yao's forehead
Cao's neck and the shoulders of Tsé Tchin
A man tall as Yu, and he wanders about in front of the East gate
        like a dog that has lost his owner.
Wrong, said Confucius, in what he says of those Emperors
        but as to the lost dog, quite correct.
He was seven days foodless in Tchin,
        the rest sick and Kung making music
"sang even more than was usual"
Honour to Yng P the bastard
Tchin and Tsai cut off Kung in the desert
        and Tcheou troops alone got him out
            Tsao fell after 25 generations
And Kung cut 3000 odes to 300
Comet from Yng star to Sin star, that is two degrees long
in the 40th year of King Ouang
Died Kung aged 73   b. c. 479

Min Kong's line was six centuries lasting
                    and there were 84 princes
Swine think of extending borders
Decent rulers of internal order
                    Fan-li sought the five lakes
Took presents but made no highways
Snow fell in midsummer
                    Apricots were in December, Mountains defend no state
nor swift rivers neither, neither Tai-hia nor Hoang-ho
Usurpations, jealousies, taxes
Greed, murder, jealousies, taxes and douanes,
338 died Hao tse Kong-sung-yang
Sout-tsin, armament racket, war propaganda.
          And Tchan-y was working for Tsin
                    brain work POLLON IDEN
and Tchao Siang called himself "Emperor of the Occident"
Sou Tsi thought it badinage
Yo-Y reduced corvées and taxes.
Thus of Kung or Confucius, and of "Hillock" his father
when he was attacking a city
his men had passed under the drop gate
And the warders then dropped it, so Hillock caught
the whole weight on his shoulder, and held till his
last man had got out.
          Of such stock was Kungfutseu.

  Chou

from CANTO LXII

Talleyrand . . . Mr A. not caught asleep by *his* cabinet
so that on the 18th of Feb. the senate recd/ the nomination of Murray
and a communication of Talleyrand's document
assuming no risk in trusting
            the professions of Talleyrand.
Not vindictive that I can remember
            though I have often been wroth
at any rate staved off a war
            roused the land to be ready
a pardon for all offenders
            (i. e. poor dutch Fries and companions)
formed own view of Hamilton's game (and his friends')
which wd/ certainly have tangled with Europe
wont to give to his conversation
            full impetus of vehement will,
charged course of Ham and his satellites
to disappointment that they hadn't
            got us entangled with Britain
defensive and offensive
            Snot, Bott, Cott left over from
Washington's cabinet
            and as for Hamilton
we may take it (my authority, ego scriptor cantilenae)
that he was the Prime snot in ALL American history
            (11th Jan. 1938, from Rapallo)
But for the clearest head in the congress
                              1774 and thereafter

                    pater patriae
        the man who at certain points
                    made us
        at certain points
                    saved us
        by fairness, honesty and straight moving

                                    ARRIBA ADAMS

Zeus lies in Ceres' bosom
Taishan is attended of loves
                    under Cythera, before sunrise
and he said: "Hay aquí mucho catolicismo — (sounded
    catoli*th*ismo)
                    y muy poco reliHión"
and he said: "Yo creo que los reyes desaparecen"
(Kings will, I think, disappear)
That was Padre José Elizondo
                    in 1906 and in 1917

or about 1917
            and Dolores said "Come pan, niño," (eat bread, me lad)
Sargent had painted her
                    before he descended
(i.e. if he descended)
            but in those days he did thumb sketches,
impressions of the Velásquez in the Museo del Prado
and books cost a peseta,
                    brass candlesticks in proportion,
hot wind came from the marshes
        and death-chill from the mountains.
And later Bowers wrote: "but such hatred,
    I had never conceived such"
and the London reds wouldn't show up his friends
                    (i.e. friends of Franco
working in London) and in Alcázar
forty years gone, they said: "Go back to the station to eat,

you can sleep here for a peseta"
            goat bells tinkled all night
            and the hostess grinned: "Eso es luto, *haw*!
mi marido es muerto"
            (it is mourning, my husband is dead)
when she gave me paper of the locanda to write on
with a black border half an inch or more deep,
      say 5/8ths,
"We call *all* foreigners frenchies"
and the egg broke in Cabranez' pocket,
            thus making history. Basil says
they beat drums for three days
till all the drumheads were busted
            (simple village fiesta)
and as for his life in the Canaries . . .
Possum observed that the local portagoose folk dance
was danced by the same dancers in divers localities
            in political welcome . . .
the technique of demonstration
            Cole studied that (not G.D.H., Horace)
"You will find" said old André Spire,
"that every man on that board (Crédit Agricole)
has a brother-in-law."
                  "You the one, I the few"
            said John Adams
speaking of fears in the abstract
      to his volatile friend Mr Jefferson.
(To break the pentameter, that was the first heave)
or as Jo Bard says: "They never speak to each other,
if it is baker and concierge visibly

it is La Rochefoucauld and de Maintenon audibly."
"Te caverò le budella"
                "La corata a te"
In less than a geological epoch
                said Henry Mencken
"Some cook, some do not cook,
        some things cannot be altered"
Ἰυγξ . . . 'εμὸν ποτί δῶμα τὸν ἄνδρα
What counts is the cultural level,
        thank Benin for this table ex packing box
        "doan yu tell no one I made it"
                from a mask fine as any in Frankfurt
"It'll get you offn th' groun"
                Light as the branch of Kuanon
And at first disappointed with shoddy
the bare ramshackle quais, but then saw the
high buggy wheels
                and was reconciled,
George Santayana arriving in the port of Boston
and kept to the end of his life that faint *thethear*
of the Spaniard
                as a grace quasi imperceptible,
as did Muss the *v* for *u* of Romagna,
and said the grief was a full act
        repeated for each new condoleress
working up to a climax.
And George Horace said he wd/ "get Beveridge" (Senator)
Beveridge wouldn't talk and he wouldn't write for the papers
but George got him by campin' in his hotel
and assailin' him at lunch breakfast an' dinner

        three articles
and my ole man went on hoein' corn
        while George was a-tellin' him,
come across a vacant lot
            where you'd occasionally see a wild rabbit
or mebbe only a loose one
        AOI!
        a leaf in the current
                        at my grates no Althea

libretto

Yet
Ere the season died a-cold
Borne upon a zephyr's shoulder
I rose through the aureate sky
            Lawes and Jenkins guard thy rest
            Dolmetsch ever be thy guest,
Has he tempered the viol's wood
To enforce   both the grave   and the acute?
Has he curved us the bowl of the lute?
            Lawes and Jenkins guard thy rest
            Dolmetsch ever be thy guest,
Hast 'ou fashioned so airy a mood
        To draw up leaf from the root?
Hast 'ou found   a cloud   so light
        As seemed neither mist nor shade?

                Then resolve me, tell me aright
                If Waller sang or Dowland played.

Your eyen two wol sleye me sodenly
I may the beauté of hem nat susteyne

And for 180 years almost nothing.

Ed ascoltando il leggier mormorio
        there came new subtlety of eyes into my tent,
whether of spirit or hypostasis,
        but what the blindfold hides
or at carnival
                        nor any pair showed anger
        Saw but the eyes and stance between the eyes,
colour, diastasis,
        careless or unaware it had not the
    whole tent's room
nor was place for the full Εἰδὼς
interpass, penetrate
        casting but shade beyond the other lights
            sky's clear
            night's sea
            green of the mountain pool
            shone from the unmasked eyes in half-mask's space.
What thou lovest well remains,
                            the rest is dross
What thou lov'st well shall not be reft from thee
What thou lov'st well is thy true heritage
Whose world, or mine or theirs
                    or is it of none?
First came the seen, then thus the palpable
        Elysium, though it were in the halls of hell,

What thou lovest well is thy true heritage
What thou lov'st well shall not be reft from thee

The ant's a centaur in his dragon world.
Pull down thy vanity, it is not man
Made courage, or made order, or made grace,
     Pull down thy vanity, I say pull down.
Learn of the green world what can be thy place
In scaled invention or true artistry,
Pull down thy vanity,
               Paquin pull down!
The green casque has outdone your elegance.

"Master thyself, then others shall thee beare"
     Pull down thy vanity
Thou art a beaten dog beneath the hail,
A swollen magpie in a fitful sun,
Half black half white
Nor knowst'ou wing from tail
Pull down thy vanity
        How mean thy hates
Fostered in falsity,
        Pull down thy vanity,
Rathe to destroy, niggard in charity,
Pull down thy vanity,
        I say pull down.

But to have done instead of not doing
        this is not vanity
To have, with decency, knocked

That a Blunt should open
   To have gathered from the air a live tradition
or from a fine old eye the unconquered flame
This is not vanity.
   Here error is all in the not done,
all in the diffidence that faltered . . .

ὕδωρ
HUDOR et Pax
Gemisto stemmed all from Neptune
      hence the Rimini bas reliefs
Sd Mr Yeats (W. B.) "Nothing affects these people
        Except our conversation"
lux enim
     ignis est accidens and,
wrote the prete in his edition of Scotus:
Hilaritas   the virtue *hilaritas*

the queen stiched King Carolus' shirts or whatever
while Erigena put greek tags in his excellent verses
      in fact an excellent poet, Paris
         toujours Pari'
            (Charles le Chauve)

     and you might find a bit of enamel
     a bit of true blue enamel
       on a metal pyx or whatever
   omnia, quae sunt, lumina sunt, or whatever

so they dug up his bones in the time of De Montfort
    (Simon)

      Le Paradis n'est pas artificiel
and Uncle William dawdling around Notre Dame

in search of whatever
               paused to admire the symbol
with Notre Dame standing inside it
Whereas in St Etienne
               or why not Dei Miracoli:
mermaids, that carving,

       in the drenched tent there is quiet
               sered eyes are at rest

       the rain beat as with colour of feldspar
       blue as the flying fish off Zoagli
pax, ὕδωρ   "ΥΔΩΡ
       the sage
delighteth in water
       the humane man has amity with the hills

as the grass grows by the weirs
               thought Uncle William   *consiros*
as the grass on the roof of St What's his name
     near "Cane e Gatto"
         soll deine Liebe sein
it would be about a-level the windows
       the grass would, or I dare say above that
       when they bless the wax for the Palio

Olim de Malatestis
       with Maria's face there in the fresco
       painted two centuries sooner,
       at least that
before she wore it

                As Montino's
in that family group of about 1820
        not wholly Hardy's material

                or πάντα 'ρει

as he was standing below the altars
            of the spirits of rain
        "When every hollow is full
            it moves forward"
        to the phantom mountain above the cloud
But in the caged panther's eyes:

                        "Nothing. Nothing that you can do . . ."

green pool, under green of the jungle,
caged: "Nothing, nothing that you can do."

Δρυάς, your eyes are like the clouds

Nor can who has passed a month in the death cells
        believe in capital punishment
No man who has passed a month in the death cells
        believes in cages for beasts

Δρυάς, your eyes are like the clouds over Taishan
        When some of the rain has fallen
        and half remains yet to fall

The roots go down to the river's edge
        and the hidden city moves upward
            white ivory under the bark

With clouds over Taishan-Chocorua
        when the blackberry ripens
and now the new moon faces Taishan
one must count by the dawn star
     Dryad, thy peace is like water
There is September sun on the pools

Plura diafana
        Heliads lift the mist from the young willows
there is no base seen under Taishan
     but the brightness of 'udor   ὕδωρ
the poplar tips float in brightness
only the stockade posts stand

And now the ants seem to stagger
          as the dawn sun has trapped their shadows,
this breath wholly covers the mountains
      it shines and divides
it nourishes by its rectitude
does no injury
overstanding the earth it fills the nine fields
             to heaven

Boon companion to equity
     it joins with the process
         lacking it, there is inanition

When the equities are gathered together
as birds alighting
it springeth up vital

If deeds be not ensheaved and garnered in the heart
there is inanition

      (have I perchance a debt to a man named Clower)

that he eat of the barley corn
and move with the seed's breath

the sun as a golden eye
          between dark cloud and the mountain

8th October:
        Si tuit li dolh elh plor
                Angold τέθνηκε
tuit lo pro, tuit lo bes
                Angold τέθνηκε

"an' doan you think he chop an' change all the time
stubborn az a mule, sah, stubborn as a MULE,
got th' eastern idea about money"
                Thus Senator Bankhead
"am sure I don't know what a man like you
        would find to *do* here"
                said Senator Borah
Thus the solons, in Washington,
on the executive, and on the country, a. d. 1939

ye spotted lambe
        that is both blacke and white
is yeven to us for the eyes' delight

and now Richardson, Roy Richardson,
        says he is different
will I mention his name?

and Demattia is checking out.
        White, Fazzio, Bedell, *benedicti*
Sarnone, two Washingtons (dark) J and M

Bassier, Starcher, H. Crowder and
no soldier he although his name is Slaughter

this day October the whateverth   Mr. Coxey
aged 91 has mentioned bonds and their
                        interest
apparently as a basis of issue
and Mr Sinc Lewis has not
          and Bartók has left us
and Mr Beard in his admirable condensation
(Mr Chas. Beard) has given one line to the currency
at about page 426 "The Young Republic"
We will be about as popular as Mr John Adams
and less widely perused
and the he leopard lay on his back playing with straw
in sheer boredom,
         (Memoirs of the Roman zoo)
                  in sheer boredom

Incense to Apollo
              Carrara
                  snow on the marble

snow-white
          against stone-white
on the mountain
and as who passed the gorges between sheer cliffs
as it might be by, is it the Garonne?
          where one walks into Spagna
that T'ao Ch'ien heard the old Dynasty's music

         as it might be at the Peach-blossom Fountain
where are smooth lawns with the clear stream
between them, silver, dividing,

and at Ho Ci'u destroyed the whole town
for hiding a woman, Κύθηρα δεινά
and as Carson the desert rat said
"when we came out we had
            80 thousand dollars' worth"
                      ("of experience")
that was from mining
         having spent their capital on equipment
but not cal'lated the time for return
and my old great aunt did likewise
with that too large hotel
but at least she saw damn all Europe
            and rode on that mule in Tangiers
                  and in general had a run for her money

like Natalie
               "perhaps more than was in it"

      Under white clouds, cielo di Pisa,
out of all this beauty something must come,

O moon my pin-up,
                     chronometer
Wei, Chi and Pi-kan
Yin had these three men full of humanitas (manhood)
            or jên²

Xaire Alessandro
                Xaire Fernando, e il Capo,
Pierre, Vidkun,
            Henriot
and as to gradations
who went out of industrials into Governments
       when the slump was in the offing
as against whom, prepense, got OUT of Imperial Chemicals
in 1938
so as not to be nourished by blood-bath?

quand vos venetz al som de l'escalina
                     ἦθος gradations
These are distinctions in clarity

ming²   these are distinctions

John Adams, the Brothers Adam
        there is our norm of spirit

our   chung¹

    whereto we may pay our
                    homage
        Saith Micah:
             Each in the name of . . .
So that looking at the sputtering tank of nicotine and
        stale whiskey

                    (on its way out)
Kumrad Koba remarked:
            "I will believe the American."
                            Berlin 1945
the last appearance of Winston P. M. in that connection
            e poi io dissi alla sorella
della pastorella dei suini, δῖα ὑφορβα:
"E questi americani?
            si conducono bene?"
ed ella: "Poco.
            Poco, poco."
ed io: "Peggio dei tedeschi?"
            ed ella: "Uguale," through the barbed wire
                    you can, said Stef (Lincoln Steffens)
do nothing with revolutionaries
        until they are at the end of their tether
and that Vandenberg has read Stalin, or Stalin, John Adams
is, at the mildest, unproven.

If the hoar frost grip thy tent
Thou wilt give thanks when night is spent.

LING[2]

Our dynasty came in because of a great sensibility.

All there by the time of I Yin

All roots by the time of I Yin.

Galileo index'd 1616,

Wellington's peace after Vaterloo

chih[3]

a gnomon,

Our science is from the watching of shadows;

That Queen Bess translated Ovid,

Cleopatra wrote of the currency,

Versus who scatter old records

ignoring the hsien[2] form

and jump to the winning side.

Père Henri Jacques still
       speaks with the sennin on Rokku,
"These people" said Mr Tcheou "should
be like brothers. They read the same books,"
       meaning chinese and japanese.
Marse Adams done tol' 'em.
The Major done told 'em
     having a First Folio (Shx) in his lock-box
could afford waiting to see it.
            "Every ... etc ...
downright corruption." "To the consumer."
     Waal, they bust the abundance
and had to pay Europe,
       an' Anatole tol' 'em:
       "no export? No need to make war."
         Ile des Pingouins,
So that Perry "opened" Japan.
Use of foreign coin until 1819.
    Exception Spanish milled dollars,
every dealer occupied in exporting them,   page 446
their exclusion an unconstitutional fraud ...
A currency of intrinsic value FOR WHICH
     They paid interest to NOBODY

                           page 446
                           column 2

LOVE, gone as lightning,
   enduring 5000 years.
Shall the comet cease moving
   or the great stars be tied in one place!
  "Consonantium demonstratrix"

        ἔφατ' Baeda
Deus est anima mundi,
   animal optimum
      et sempiternum.
Tempus est ubique,
     non motus
        in vesperibus orbis.
Expergesci thalamis, gravat serpella nimbus
Mist weighs down the wild thyme plants.
  "In favour of the whole people." "They repeat"
    said Delcroix
Van Buren unsmearing Talleyrand,
    Adams to Rush before that, in 1811
And there were guilds in Byzantium.
  "Not political," Dante says, a
     "compagnevole animale"
Even if some do coagulate into cities
    πόλις, πολιτική
reproducteur,
    contribuable. Paradis peint
but πολεύω meaning to plough
  πολύγλωσσος

98

There were many sounds in that oak-wood.
Benton: when there was plenty of metal,
Van Buren already desmearing Talleyrand
J. A. "the whole people (devaluation)."
Alexander paid the debts of his soldiery
      And over an arch in Vicenza, the stemma,
the coat of arms, stone: "Lapo, ghibelline exile."
      "Who knows but I also from some vento di siepe?"
six centuries later "degli Uberti."
            Queen of Heaven bring her repose
            Κάδμου θυγάτηρ
            bringing light per diafana
λευκὸς Λευκόθοε
                  white foam, a sea-gull
And damn it there were men even in my time
      Nicoletti, Ramperti, Desmond Fitzgerald
            (the one alive in 1919)
That the crystal wave mount to flood surge

近　　chin⁴

平　　hu¹

仁　　jên²

      The light there almost solid.
YAO'S worry: to find a successor

一　　i¹·⁵·

人　　jên²

& the three years peace we owe Windsor
          '36 - '39
As from the terrace, Saint Bertrand
       to southward from Montrejeau
Elder Lightfoot is not downhearted,
   Elder Lightfoot is cert'nly

                 not

                    downhearted,
He observes a design in the Process.
Miss Ida by the bars in the jail house
          "de Nantes
il y a un prisonnier," periplum
from Madrid more than 40 years earlier,
          Carrière show in Paris,
"Bret" in la rue Grande Chaumière.
      the jap girl: "Mais Rembrandt"
        in ecstasy
And the *russe*

        bringing all the "Smoke" of Turgenev.
"Are" as Uncle William said "the daughters of Memory"
"Pirandello,

       because that is the sort of thing that . . .
that does go on in one's mind."

           Whose mind?
Among all these twerps and Pulitzer sponges
     no voice for the Constitution,
No objection to the historic blackout.

   "My bikini is worth yr/ raft." Said Leucothea
And if I see her not
No sight is worth the beauty of my thought.

The immense cowardice of advertised literati
    & Elsa Kassandra, "the Baroness"
von Freitag etc. sd/ several true things
in the old days /
            driven nuts,
Well, of course, there was a certain strain
    on the gal in them days in Manhattan
the principle of non-acquiescence
                 laid a burden.

Dinklage, where art thou,
    with, or without, your *von*?
You said the teeth of the black troops
    reminded you of the boar-hunt,
I think yr/ first boar hunt, but
The black prisoners had such a nice way with children,
Also what's his name who spent the night in the air
caught in the mooring-ropes.
        Lone rock for sea-gull
who can, in any case, rest on water!
Do not Hindoos
        lust after vacuity?
With the Gardasee at our disposition.
"O World!"
      said Mr Beddoes.
"Something *there*,"
        sd/ Santayana.
Responsus:
     Not stasis/
       at least not in our immediate vicinage.
a hand without face cards,

the enormous organized cowardice.
And there is something decent in the universe
    if I can feel all this, *dicto millesimo*
At the age of whatever.
I suppose St. Hilary looked at an oak-leaf.
(vine-leaf ? Saint Denys —
    (spelled Dionisio)
Dionisio et Eleutherio.
Dionisio et Eleutherio
        "the brace of 'em
that Calvin never blacked out" —
                        en l'Isle.)
That the wave crashed, whirling the raft, then
Tearing the oar from his hand,
                        broke mast and yard-arm
And he was drawn down under wave,
        The wind tossing,
Notus, Boreas,
            as it were thistle-down.
Then Leucothea had pity,
                    "mortal once
Who now is a sea-god:
                    νόστου
γαίης Φαιήκων, ..."

from CANTO XCIX

And if your kids don't study, that's your fault.
Tell 'em. Don't kid yourself, and don't lie.
In statement, answer; in conversation
                    not with sissified fussiness (chiao¹)
                always want your own way.
Let 'em ask before taking action;
That there be no slovenly sloppiness
                    between goodman & wife.
Gt. is gt. . Little is little;
With friends one is one
                    2 is 2
Not to lie out of heedlessness
                let alone out of trickery
Fitting the tone to their words
                    as water goes over the mill-wheel.
Dress 'em in folderols
                    and feed 'em with dainties,
In the end they will sell out the homestead.
Taxes, for public utility,
                    a share of a product,
People have bodies
                    ergo they sow and reap,
Soldiers also have bodies,
                    take care of the body as implement,
It is useful,
To shield you from floods and rascality.

Born of the blue sky and a wild cat
                    Cloud in thunder and rain,
Basalt, the stone gong
            "if," as Yao said: "you can keep these two lovelies
                    in order!"
You forget the timing of budgets
                that is to say you probably don't even know that
Officials exist in time. You are fairly unconscious
            Hsiang i hsiang
but in muddle and incomprehension   14.5
            the contemplation of outlay
                        hsiao^4
tsou^4 memorial
the k'ao ch'eng is according to harvest,
the tax as a share of something produced.

You can waste more on tips and wangles
                (Thiers a progress from Talleyrand,
less brain and more morals)
            PANURGIA? SOPHIA:
                what will *not* do,
Are distinguished by what they will not—
Cannibals wd/ resist canneries, Ersatz
    a given state of enlightenment, scienza
                    XIV
Thru the ten voices of the tradition
                the land has been ploughed
                    t'ien^2 ti^4
& there have been taxes in kind, and by (liang^2) measure
This is important

      as to the scope of such taxes
all Courts have levied them
        the right pattern of levy is yang[4] cheng[1]
                    id est: for use
not a fountain of folderols
for top popinjays.
            Wranglings won't get you out of it
High & low, top & under
            INCORPORATE
& in one body.
The ups are not malevolent,
         you might consider their complications;
Dykes for flood-water,
           someone must build 'em;
             must plan 'em,
By the ten mouths of the tradition:
              have peace
Meaning get rid of criminality. Catch 'em!

Ancestral spring making breed, a pattern
Yong (2. 2. 3)
"12 inches, guinea an inch!" said Elkin Mathews
        in regard to Courtney's review.
The State is corporate
        as with pulse in its body
& with Chou rite at the root of it
The root is thru all of it,
        a tone in all public teaching:
This is not a work of fiction

nor yet of one man:

The six kinds of action, filial, reciprocal,
Sincerity from of old until now,

holding together

Not shallow in verbal usage

nor in dissociations;

Shallow prides, feeble dissociations,
And spend their time slanting rumours;

keep things off-center, slander and blabber-mouth;

Rail; scold and ructions; *manesco*

and the whole family suffers.

The whole tribe is from one man's body,

what other way can you think of it?

The surname, and the 9 arts.

The father's word is compassion;
The son's, filiality.
The brother's word: mutuality;
The younger's word: deference.

Small birds sing in chorus,
Harmony is in the proportion of branches

as clarity (chao[1]).

Compassion, tree's root and water-spring;

The state: order, inside a boundary;
Law: reciprocity.

What is statute save reciprocity?
One village in order,

one valley will reach the four seas.

CHÊN, *yo el Rey*, wish you to think of this EDICT.

4.

Having heard that provisions are the root of the people
                              (logistica)
                    nung
                              sang
To sprout in season
                    and have trees for your silk-worms,
One big chap not plow,
                    one female not weave
Can mean shortage,
From of old the sovereign likes plowing
& the Empress tends trees with reverence;
                    Nor shrink from the heat of labour

              chao⁴   兆   an omen

The plan is in nature
                    rooted
Coming from earth, times (ch'ang²) respected
Their powers converging
                    chu⁴ assemble
There is a must at the root of it
                    not one man's mere power,
Thru high-low, parch and dampness
High, dry for panicled millet
Damp, low for rice (non-glutinous) and paddy
        wu² mu ch'i² ying² pei⁴ li⁴
                              (interest)
not for a quick buck at high interest
the legal rate does not exhaust things
              (Byzance did better)

Don't burn to abandon production and go into trading,
Dig up root to chase branches
vide Michelet & Ambrose "De Tobia"
The rate in Byzance was lower,
as can continuous far
(*que ça doure*)
Established that everybody got some education
AND you had literate Confucians
in the bureaucracy,
Focus of men of ability solidified our good customs.
Shut out graceful bigots
and moderate thundering phalloi
(this is a mistranslation)
Strong, weak, to one coöperation,
our SAGE FOREBEAR examined to
stimulate anagogico
and more especially magnified schools—
everything that wd/ bring up esprit de corps

en[1] 恩

trained his officers not to slant government
and to be ready for anything.
1st/ the basic in his own practice,
then village usage
to see what style for the casting
Filiality and fraternity are the root,
Talents to be considered as branches.
Precise terminology is the first implement,
dish and container,
After that the 9 arts.

AND study the classic books,
                    the straight history
                                all of it candid.
Be friends with straight officers
                        chiao[1] communicate,
They *are* your communications,
                a hasty chirrp may raise ruin.
You, soldiers, civilians,
                are not headed to be professors.
The basis is man,
                and the rectification of officers
But the four TUAN
                    are from nature
        jên, i, li, chih
Not from descriptions in the schoolhouse;
They are the scholar's job,
                the gentleman's and the officer's.

There is worship in plowing
                and equity in the weeding hoe,
A field marshal can be literate.
                Might we see it again in our day!

All I want is a generous spirit in customs
            1st/ honest man's heart demands sane curricula
                (no, that is not textual)
Let him analyze the trick programs
                    and fake foundations
The fu jen receives heaven, earth, middle
                    and grows.

You cannot leave these things out.
            οὐ θέλει ἔην εἰς κόσμον
but from at least here is the Charta Magna
I shall have to learn a little greek to keep up with this
            but so will you, drratt you.
"They want to bust out of the kosmos"

                        accensio

Anselm versus damn Rufus
"Ugly? a bore,

            Pretty, a whore!"

                        brother Anselm is pessimistic,
digestion weak,

            but had a clear line on the Trinity, and
by sheer grammar: Essentia

                  feminine

                        Immaculata

Immaculabile. Ambrose:

            "First treason: shepherd to flock."
            and they want it apocryphal.
Franks: ten years' exemption from taxes

            Valentinian to oust the Alani
            and then Omnia Gallia, Faramond, 425
Pepin, over an altar to Zagreus,

            Ethelbald: tax exemptions
                  Charles to Offa, a belt, one hungarian sword.
Quendrida bumped off brother Kenelm,

            Egbert left local laws.

"Looping the light over my shoulder,"
                    (Charles of the Suevi)
          "Drew me over fiery mountains" /
As is left in Hariulf's Chronicle. Thus dreamed it.
For a thousand years savages against maniacs
                              and vice versa.
Alfred sorted out hundreds; tithings,
          They probably murdered Erigena,
                    Athelstan gon yilden rere, after 925
                    Aunt Ethelfled had been literate,
                              Canute for alleviation of Alp tolls
                              Gerbert at the astrolabe
                                        better than Ptolemy,
A tenth tithe and circet of corn.
With a Crommelyn at the breech-block
                    or a del Valle,
This is what the swine haven't got
                    with their
                              πανουργία

Guido had read the Proslogion
                    as had, presumably, Villon.

from CANTO CVIII

ELIZABETH
                    Angliae amor,
                    ad valorem reducta.
          To take wood to melt ore
                    non extat memoria
                              . . . ardendam, fundendam
          & souls of the dead defrauded
                              35 Edward
          send or cause to be sent out of the
                                        Kingdom
          and that the seal be in custody of four men dignioribus
                                                  & the prior
          alien abbots may visit;
                         not export
                                   by means whereof daily almes was decayed
          . . . to Paragots alone
                         10 000 marks
                                   alienigenae superiores
          the brocars of Rome promote caitifes
                                   learning decayeth
                                                  Rot., parl 50 E. 3
          damnable customs introduc of new in Roma.
          That grosbois is oak, ash, elm,
                                   beech, horsbeche & hornbeam
          but of acorns tithe shall be paid
          For every lamb a penny
                         time out of mind
                                   one lira per sheep nel Tirolo

sale must be in place overt
        not in a backe-room
& between sun-up & sun-down
                        dies solaris
ut pena ad paucos
                metus ad omnes perveniat
of 2 rights the more ancient preferred
                caveat emptor
HORSFAIRE from 10 of the clock before noon
                        until sunset
the queenes dominions
                Phil, Mar
Colour, with one speciall mark at the least
        of every such horse, mare, colt, gelding
                on paine of default 40 shillings
        ridden openly for one hour
                and after 10 in the morning
as might be for Cadillacs, Fords & such other
                ridden, led, walked or kept standing
& in free markets to the book-keeper one penny
                                        no toll

Coke, Iong Ching
        responsabili
par cretance del ewe which is
        french for floodwater.
Who for bridges
        reparando;
For every new cottage 4 acres
                Stat. de 31 Eliz.
                        Angliae amor.

Wing like feldspar

                and the foot-grip firm to hold balance

Green yellow the sunlight, more rapid,

Azaleas by snow slope.

Afraid he will balk and not sign mobilization,

             got, said Monro, to get rid of him

                     (Eddie)

He has been around in the hospitals

                Jury trial was in Athens

Who for bridges

       reparando

For every new cottage 4 acres

       Stat. de 31 Eliz.

             Angliae amor

And false stone not to be set in true gold

to the king only, to put value

       and to make price of the quantity

auxy soit signe teste leopard

Clear deep off Taormina

       high cliff and azure beneath it

form is cut in the lute's neck, tone is from the bowl

Oak boughs alone over Selloi

         This wing, colour of feldspar

             phyllotaxis

Over wicket gate

    INO Ινώ Kadmeia

Erigena, Anselm,
                the fight thru Herbert and Rémusat
Helios,
          Καλλιαστράγαλος Ino Kadmeia,
San Domenico, Santa Sabina,
                              Sta Maria Trastevere;
                                   in Cosmedin
Le chapeau melon de St Pierre
          You in the dinghy (piccioletta) astern there!

The scientists are in terror
      and the European mind stops
Wyndham Lewis chose blindness
      rather than have his mind stop.
Night under wind mid garofani,
      the petals are almost still
Mozart, Linnaeus, Sulmona,
When one's friends hate each other
      how can there be peace in the world?
Their asperities diverted me in my green time.
A blown husk that is finished
      but the light sings eternal
a pale flare over marshes
      where the salt hay whispers to tide's change
Time, space,
      neither life nor death is the answer.
And of man seeking good,
      doing evil.
In meiner Heimat
      where the dead walked
      and the living were made of cardboard.

CANTO CXVI

Came Neptunus
        his mind leaping
                like dolphins,
These concepts the human mind has attained.
To make Cosmos—
To achieve the possible—
Muss., wrecked for an error,
But the record
        the palimpsest—
a little light
        in great darkness—
cuniculi—
An old "crank" dead in Virginia.
Unprepared young burdened with records,
The vision of the Madonna
          above the cigar butts
            and over the portal.
"Have made a mass of laws"
               (mucchio di leggi)
Litterae nihil sanantes
          Justinian's,
a tangle of works unfinished.

I have brought the great ball of crystal;
        who can lift it?
Can you enter the great acorn of light?
        But the beauty is not the madness

Tho' my errors and wrecks lie about me.
And I am not a demigod,
I cannot make it cohere.
If love be not in the house there is nothing.
The voice of famine unheard.
How came beauty against this blackness,
Twice beauty under the elms—
        To be saved by squirrels and bluejays?
          "plus j'aime le chien"
Ariadne.
     Disney against the metaphysicals,
and Laforgue more than they thought in him,
Spire thanked me in proposito
And I have learned more from Jules
              (Jules Laforgue) since then
deeps in him,
     and Linnaeus.
          chi crescerà i nostri—
but about that terzo
     third heaven,
        that Venere,
again is all "paradiso"
    a nice quiet paradise
        over the shambles,
and some climbing
        before the take-off,
to "see again,"
the verb is "see," not "walk on"
i.e. it coheres all right
        even if my notes do not cohere.

Many errors,
                    a little rightness,
to excuse his hell
                        and my paradiso.
And as to why they go wrong,
                            thinking of rightness
And as to who will copy this palimpsest?
            al poco giorno
                                ed al gran cerchio d'ombra
But to affirm the gold thread in the pattern
                                (Torcello)
al Vicolo d'oro
                (Tigullio).
To confess wrong without losing rightness:
Charity I have had sometimes,
                    I cannot make it flow thru.
A little light, like a rushlight
                    to lead back to splendour.